W9-BNL-108

When Larry Burkett's *Debt-Free Living* was first published in 1989, I could have been one of the horror story case studies that opened the book. Coming out of my own bankruptcy at the time, I was on a mission to discover how money really works. *Debt-Free Living* was a light in my darkness, giving voice to a lifetime of common-sense financial principles that I had largely ignored. Now, twenty years later, I believe there has never been a better time for the time-honored, godly principles of this book to make a comeback.

> —DAVE RAMSEY is the bestselling author of *The Total Money Makeover*, a nationally syndicated radio talk show host, and host of The Dave Ramsey Show on the Fox Business Network.

It is a privilege for me to endorse the revised *Debt-Free Living* by the person who made an impact on his world like no other. Larry's life message is sorely needed today. As he would say, "God's principles of finances are always right, always relevant, and will never change."

> —RON BLUE is a bestselling author and president of Kingdom Advisors

Sometimes it seemed as though Larry Burkett could see around corners. He certainly saw things long before the rest of us. That's why his warnings about the dangers of debt and the direction of our economy still ring true. Indeed, the turmoil of recent years has given even greater force to his insights. Of course, as Larry would say with genuine humility, "All I do is plagiarize Scripture." He saw his role as simply trying to convey that God's Word is true and that the Lord can be trusted. Indeed, that's what *Debt-Free Living* is all about.

> —AUSTIN PRYOR is founder and president, SoundMindInvesting.com

DEBT-FREE LIVING

Eliminating Debt in a New Economy

LARRY BURKETT

MOODY PUBLISHERS

CHICAGO

© 2010 CROWN FINANCIAL MINISTRIES

1999 edition © by CHRISTIAN FINANCIAL CONCEPTS

All rights reserved. No part of this book may be reproduced in any form without permission in writing from the publisher, except in the case of brief quotations embodied in critical articles or reviews.

All Scripture quotations, unless otherwise indicated, are taken from the *Holy Bible, New International Version®*. NIV®. Copyright © 1973, 1978, 1984 by Biblica, Inc.™ Used by permission of Zondervan. All rights reserved.

Scripture quotations marked ESV are taken from *The Holy Bible, English Standard Version*. Copyright © 2000, 2001 by Crossway Bibles, a division of Good News Publishers. Used by permission. All rights reserved.

Editor of 2010 edition: Pam Pugh
Cover design: Dog Eared Design
Cover image: iStockphoto
Interior design: Smartt Guys design

Library of Congress Cataloging-in-Publication Data

Burkett, Larry.

  Debt-free living : eliminating debt in a new economy / Larry Burkett.

  p. cm.

  Includes bibliographical references.

  ISBN 978-0-8024-2566-9

  1. Finance, Personal. 2. Debt. I. Title.

  HG179.B83495 2010

  332.024'02—dc22

2009045081

We hope you enjoy this book from Moody Publishers. Our goal is to provide high-quality, thought-provoking books and products that connect truth to your real needs and challenges. For more information on other books and products written and produced from a biblical perspective, go to www.moodypublishers.com or write to:

Moody Publishers
820 N. LaSalle Boulevard
Chicago, IL 60610

3 5 7 9 10 8 6 4 2

Printed in the United States of America

CONTENTS

PREFACE TO THE 2010 EDITION

Larry Burkett's desire was to teach Christians what God's Word says about finances and to show them how to practically apply these principles to their lives.

From 1977 when he founded Christian Financial Concepts—now Crown Financial Ministries—to the present, countless books have been written on the subject of money, seminars have been taught, and an abundance of information is now readily available through the Internet. Still, Larry's basic principles hold true.

Because today's financial climate has changed since Larry first wrote *Debt-Free Living*, we thought it worthwhile to revise and update his enduring work. We have added a couple of new stories, reworked the original ones to reflect contemporary life, updated information, and more. A new section on books and online resources is included.

In keeping with the author's first-person voice and his teachings, we offer you this fresh look at Larry Burkett's *Debt-Free Living*.

—MOODY PUBLISHERS, APRIL 2010

FOREWORD

Our world has changed significantly since Larry Burkett first penned the words of this book two decades ago, and this latest version of *Debt-Free Living* has been updated to be current with many of those changes.

As the old saying goes, "The more things change, the more they stay the same." However, in the case of debt, personal and national levels have not remained constant—they have skyrocketed. But what has not changed is the source of wisdom that Larry drew upon to lead the reader into a life free from financial slavery: God's Word. It remains relevant, practical, and effective for bringing about the spiritual and financial transformation that we need.

We as Christians are called to be aliens and strangers in this world. Today, more than ever, we must heed the warnings contained in these pages and take action. Larry's classic work will give you the motivation and the process to follow so that you can live without debt regardless of how impossible that may seem now.

As you read these pages, my hope is that you'll resolve to change course—to reset your heart and mind and discover the life-transforming freedom of living without debt. If you do that, Larry's goal in writing this book will have been realized. You'll be liberated, and you will grow closer to Christ and His purposes for your life.

On your journey toward debt-free living, you may need help. I invite you to stay in touch with us at Crown.org. It will be our joy to serve and encourage you.

CHUCK BENTLEY
CEO, Crown Financial Ministries
1 Corinthians 1:9

PART ONE:

STORIES *of* PEOPLE
WHO FELL INTO DEBT...

C H A P T E R

BEN and NAOMI:
WHAT *They*
DIDN'T KNOW

Ben and Naomi were both from middle-income families. They grew up in the suburban area of Chicago and did their share of chores around the house.

Naomi's father was a practical person who kept the household records and distributed the money. He budgeted an amount for Naomi's mother to manage the household. He paid all the other bills and gave Naomi a modest allowance. Naomi was required to work for a portion of her clothing and entertainment money.

In Ben's family the distribution of tasks was different. His mother handled the checkbook and paid the bills. His father never got involved with family finances, except when he wanted to buy something. Then he simply wrote a check for the amount he needed. That habit caused some terrible fights, since he never bothered to record his check amounts. Ben could almost always go to his dad and get money when he needed it. When he did this, Ben's father usually told him not to tell his mother, because she would have a fit. Ben's father worked hard on his job, even picking up overtime whenever he could, and believed that the money he earned was his to spend as he wished.

Ben held several part-time jobs while he was growing up but rarely stayed at any for longer than a few weeks. Like his father, he believed that the money he made was his to spend as he desired. When he was in the twelfth grade, his father bought him a nice car, and his mother blew up about it because she hadn't been consulted.

When Ben started college, he was encouraged to apply for student aid and government loans. He completed two years of college while living at home but never really decided on a field of study. He took a summer job as an equipment operator with a local power district and received an offer to stay on permanently, which he accepted, rather than finishing his college degree.

He and Naomi dated for nearly a year after they met in college. When Ben took his permanent job, he asked Naomi to marry him, with the understanding that she would finish college and go into advertising and marketing.

Neither Ben nor Naomi received any detailed instructions from their parents about marriage. It was assumed that the pastor of Naomi's church would provide the counseling they needed. Indeed, the pastor did require several sessions in which they discussed sex, communication, and spiritual values. Once he asked Ben if he would be able to support a family, to which Ben replied, "Yes, sir, I make a good living at the Evanston Power District. We'll be all right."

The pastor never pursued the subject further. So having completed what they thought were the requirements for marriage, Ben and Naomi were married.

◑ ◑ ◑

The seeds of financial collapse were planted early in Ben and Naomi Wister's marriage. When they were married, she was twenty-one and he was twenty-two, and neither one knew much about financial matters. Their plans were simple—they would delay having children for five years. Naomi would use that time to finish college and get established in her career. After that, they would begin a family. There was some thought that Ben might go back to college someday to finish up his degree, but that was only a vague idea.

But after living in an apartment for five months, Ben decided that it didn't make any sense to keep throwing money away on rent. Some of the guys at work had told him he was losing all the tax breaks the government allowed homeowners. "Get yourself a house and start building some equity," was their advice.

Ben and Naomi began to look for a house they could buy. They found one that was near their price range, but the bank wouldn't finance it on the basis of his income alone. So during the summer college break Naomi took a job with a local product design company, part-time so she could return to college. Based on their combined incomes, they signed to buy the home. With their credit card and store credit, they were able to furnish it and buy the appliances they needed. There was enough available credit on their card to enjoy nice dinners, evenings at the movies, and sporting events.

They didn't have the down payment, so Ben's dad cosigned for a loan through his credit union. The couple did not include this amount as a loan on their mortgage application. The monthly house payments required more than half of Ben's take-home pay at the time. Almost immediately they were in financial trouble from the payments alone. With the insurance, taxes, and utilities added, Ben and Naomi were on the road to debt without realizing it.

After the first month, Ben was unable to make the payment on the credit union loan. When it was sixty days delinquent, the credit union had the payments deducted automatically, according to their written agreement. Ben's father, the cosigner, was sent a written notice of collection proceedings against him for the two months in arrears. When he received the notice, he hit the roof and stormed over to Ben and Naomi's to confront the issue.

By that point, Naomi had gone back to school. Since Ben took care of paying the bills, she hadn't realized they were behind. When she found out, she was devastated. Ben's dad demanded that they pay the past-due bill.

When Ben told him they couldn't, his dad suggested that Naomi get a full-time job.

"Ben, I can't see any way that we can keep this house," Naomi said. "Maybe we should try to sell it. I really don't want to have to drop out of school now."

"We won't have to sell the house," Ben replied emphatically. "I can get a loan on the car to catch up the payments. I'm due for a raise pretty soon; then we'll have enough to make it."

"What if the raise doesn't come through?" Naomi asked.

"You don't need to worry. Trust me; everything's going to work out."

So Naomi put the subject of finances out of her mind. But she couldn't shake the nagging feeling of impending disaster.

Ben negotiated a loan on his car for enough to catch up the credit union payment with some left over. He used that to buy a Blu-Ray disc player, reasoning they could have home entertainment instead of going out.

When Ben received his next check with the loan payment taken out, he was shocked. His net pay for the first pay period of the month was far less than he was counting on. He had already mailed the house payment, anticipating his pay, and he realized that the check probably wouldn't clear. Sure enough, the bank alerted him by e-mail and also mailed a statement that the check to the mortgage company had been paid, but their checking account was being charged for insufficient funds. Ben and Naomi were appalled at the daily fee for being in the red.

Not knowing what else to do, Ben called a local loan company that advertised immediate second mortgage loans for homeowners.

"Ben, I absolutely will not sign to get a second mortgage on this house," Naomi stated. "We can't pay the bills we have now!"

"There's nothing else we can do," Ben said, raising his voice. "We have to pay the mortgage. We don't want to foreclose."

"I don't care if we do," Naomi said, beginning to cry. "I don't think I can take much more of this." Then she added, "I'm going out for a while. I just need to get away and think."

With that, Naomi went walking and wound up at her parents' house. When Naomi's dad came home that evening, he said, "Hi—I didn't expect to see you. You don't look happy. What's the problem?"

"Oh, Daddy, we're in such a financial mess, and I can't get Ben to be honest with me. We seem to get into more trouble every month."

Naomi's father was wise enough to call Ben and ask him to come over and talk. Ben explained the problem of the credit union payment being taken out of the first of the month's paycheck, when he thought it would be taken out of the second check. Ben assured Naomi's father it was all a misunderstanding and that he would be able to make the adjustment the next month.

Rather than allow them to take out a second mortgage, Naomi's dad decided to lend them the money himself. He just asked that Ben pay back the loan as soon as he could. Ben assured him that he would do so and that it would be no longer than two months.

Even a casual observer could see at this point that giving Ben and Naomi more money was not the answer. But it's often much easier to see the truth in someone else's life than it is in your own. Certainly Ben wasn't trying to deceive anyone. He just didn't have enough information about the way finances worked to make an intelligent decision.

The loan from Naomi's father didn't solve any problems. It merely delayed the inevitable. Within a couple of months, bills were backing up again. Creditors were calling day and night. It was almost impossible for Naomi to concentrate on her schoolwork. For the first time in her life she began to let her grades slip. That put additional pressure on her, especially when her father called her cell to chide her about her midterm grades. "Naomi, we're glad to help out and pay your college tuition and buy your books, but we expect you to do your part," her father said. "If you don't keep your grades up, we'll stop helping. What's the matter? You're capable of doing better work."

Naomi was shattered. She had always had the approval of her parents, and now they were putting pressure on her too. An event that very evening became the final straw. She came home at about 6:00 p.m. from classes, almost on the verge of tears because of the earlier discussion with her father. She opened the door, flipped on the light switch and—nothing happened. She made her way to the dining room and tried that switch. Still nothing. Finally she realized that their power had been turned off.

She found a flashlight and began to look through the desk in their bedroom, where she found two delinquent notices that warned that their electricity would be turned off if the bill wasn't paid immediately. She also found similar notices from the gas and water companies. She sat there in the dark, shaking, until Ben came home.

When Ben came in she heard, "Naomi, what's the matter with the lights?"

"I'll tell you what's the matter! You haven't paid the bill, and they've turned our power off. That's what's the matter! And . . . I found notices from the other utilities too. Ben, what's going on? Can't we even keep up with the utility bills?"

"I'm sorry. I meant to pay them, but there wasn't enough money in the last paycheck. I'll try to get caught up next paycheck."

"It's always the next paycheck with you. But we never seem to have enough money to catch up. I'm going to quit school and get a full-time job. I just can't live like this anymore."

"I'm really sorry . . . but I think you're right. If you could just work for a while until we get caught up, it really would help. You should be able to go back next fall. I've got another raise coming that will help a lot then."

Naomi quit school and was able to move up to full-time hours with Wagner Design. She had been accustomed to tithing her income, as she had done before she got married, but Ben said they couldn't afford to do it. He was supported in that decision by both sets of parents, who felt it would be better to pay off some of the debts first.

For several months things seemed to get better financially, and her relationship with Ben even improved. They had some extra money to go out periodically, and Naomi was able to buy a used car so she would not be dependent on Ben to get back and forth to work.

Then Naomi began to feel nauseated in the mornings. When she missed her period, she wondered if she could be pregnant. She hadn't been disciplined about taking the birth control pills her doctor had prescribed. A home pregnancy test confirmed her suspicion: she was pregnant.

She thought about Ben's reaction and the fact that not only would a baby curtail her education, but would also greatly reduce her ability to work. She felt like she was in a box with no way out. The thought of an abortion briefly flitted through her mind, but she discarded it. Her strong Christian background would not allow her to do such a thing. But now she understood the terrible temptation that money pressures created for others who found themselves in the same situation.

"Pregnant? No!" Ben exclaimed when Naomi told him. "How could you be so stupid, Naomi? All you had to do was take your pills and you wouldn't have gotten pregnant."

"Do you think I got pregnant on purpose?" Naomi yelled back. "I don't like this any more than you do, but there is nothing I can do about it now."

Ben stormed out of their bedroom. Naomi collapsed on the bed in tears. She had always thought she'd be excited to become a mother, but this wasn't the right time. She felt guilty about getting pregnant and anxious about the future.

How will we ever be able to pay for a baby? she wondered. *If I stop working, we won't even be able to pay the bills we have now.*

The rest of that evening Naomi stayed in the bedroom and Ben stayed downstairs. He began to feel guilty about his reaction to Naomi and decided to apologize. But by the time he went upstairs she was asleep.

Naomi tried to continue to work, but morning sickness forced her to miss more and more days. Finally, her supervisor called her in to confront the issue.

"Naomi, I know you've had a tough time with this pregnancy, but you've missed six days in the last two weeks. We need someone who can do the work. Why don't you take a month's leave of absence and stay home? I'd like to keep you, but maybe I can hire a temp for a few weeks. If you're doing better, then come back and see me, and we'll try to bring you back."

"Oh, Melanie, that's thoughtful, but I can't afford to stay home," Naomi replied. "We're—I can't really talk about it, but things are pretty tight financially. I have to work, or we can't keep up with our bills. Sometimes I don't see how we'll ever get caught up."

Melanie Moore grew thoughtful, then said, "If you're that strapped, maybe you and Ben ought to see about filing for bankruptcy. You're not going to be able to work while you're so sick. And if you continue the way you're going, you will ruin your health and the baby's too."

"Bankruptcy?" Naomi said. "I never envisioned us having to do anything like that."

"My husband's an attorney," Melanie replied. "I can assure you, it's no stigma to file for bankruptcy. Here's his card. At least talk it over with Ben and give my husband, Joe, a call if you'd like to look into it."

That evening Naomi was quiet through dinner. Ben sensed something new was on her mind, but he dreaded asking what it was. Their relationship had been so tense since Naomi told him she was pregnant that they rarely spoke to each other without getting into some kind of argument. Finally, he spoke up. "What's wrong now, Naomi? You have barely said two words since I got home."

"I lost my job today," she replied matter-of-factly. "Well, I was put on leave for a month. Unpaid."

"Why? What happened?"

"Melanie Moore said I was taking too much time off, and they needed someone who is more consistent."

"They can't do that. It's illegal, isn't it?" Ben's reaction was from fear, as much as anger.

"Well, they did it," Naomi replied. "They're willing to try to bring me back when I can work again. But Melanie is right: if I keep up this pace, it may hurt the baby."

"But what are we going to do?" Ben said in despair. "We just bought your car, and we can barely make ends meet even when you work."

"Melanie suggested that we file for bankruptcy protection," Naomi replied. "She said her husband is an attorney who handles bankruptcies for couples like us all the time. But I'm not sure I want that kind of thing on my record."

"It's my record, too," Ben asserted. "We've got a lot of credit card debt along with the house and cars. We can't keep going like we are. Something's got to give."

"My mom and dad never would have had to do anything like this," Naomi answered, handing Ben the business card her supervisor had given her. "It's embarrassing."

"In a situation like ours, you do what you have to do, Naomi. It boils down to one thing: survival."

Under provisions of the 2005 bankruptcy law, Ben and Naomi were required to meet for ninety minutes with a credit counselor in their judicial district. They also had to attend classes on managing money—at their expense. In addition, the law required them to take a two-part means test, which evaluated their ability to repay their unsecured debt and compared their income to their state's median income.

In a meeting with Melanie's husband, Joe Moore, they learned that the amount of debt they hoped to eliminate through bankruptcy would not be as great as they initially thought. "Based on the results of your means test, you don't qualify for a Chapter 7 bankruptcy, which eliminates the greatest level of debt," Joe said as he looked at Ben and Naomi's paperwork. "It looks like you'll have to apply for Chapter 13."

"What does that mean?" Ben asked.

"Chapter 13 involves a repayment plan that can last up to five years," Joe replied. "Debts that the court includes in the plan will have to be repaid. The good news is, you don't have to repay the debts that aren't included."

Naomi considered the attorney's words. She didn't want bankruptcy but saw no other way out of her situation. Her chair felt hard to the point of being unbearable. She shifted right, then left, trying to find a more comfortable position. Thoughts of friends asking questions about her situation raced through her mind. She wondered if there was a way to keep it secret. Probably not. In a matter of months, everyone would know. She wondered how life might have been different if she and Ben had never bought the house, if they had waited another year to get married, if she hadn't gotten pregnant . . . At that point, Ben said something that completely blew her away.

"Well, in our case, I think bankruptcy's an answer to prayer. I don't know what Naomi and I would do without it, especially with her losing her job and a baby on the way. I see no reason not to go ahead with the Chapter 13."

"There's still the matter of the fees," Joe said, looking over the paperwork. "You seemed to indicate in an earlier discussion that they might be a problem."

"It's a lot of money, for sure."

"I know it's tough," the attorney replied as he closed the couple's file. "The 2005 law created more liability, and more work, for law firms. Of course, this required us to increase our costs."

Naomi picked up her purse off the floor in anticipation of leaving. She and Ben hadn't discussed the cost of bankruptcy or much of anything else. The financial pressure on their marriage was killing their communication. She slid to the front of her seat, ready to get up and leave, certain that Ben would do the same. She knew her parents wouldn't loan them the money for bankruptcy, and chances were that his parents wouldn't, either. She held out her hand to the attorney. "Joe, thanks so much for trying to help us. Looks like we're out of options."

"Well . . . not exactly," Ben said. "My parents have agreed to cover the cost."

Naomi shot an angry look at her husband. Once again, he had failed to communicate. "Ben, if you're talking about another loan, I'm not for it."

"Not this time." He reached out and put his hand on hers. "We don't have to pay them back. Dad and Mom want us to have a fresh start. I've assured them that we're going to get a grip on our spending."

"How long have you known this?"

"Dad called me on my cell phone last week when I was at work. I was going to tell you, but then I got busy and forgot. You know how it goes."

No, I don't know how it goes! Naomi thought as Ben gave her another reminder of his carelessness. She wanted to give him a piece of her mind, but not in front of the attorney. "I wish you'd told me," she said. "When you do things like this, I feel completely left out."

"I'm sorry, honey," Ben replied. "Right now, I'm stressed . . . we both are. But after this bankruptcy goes through, things are going to get better."

"You're going to see a big difference," Joe interjected. "And I think it was a wise decision for your parents to help, Ben. With your commitment to get control of your spending and pay what the court requires, you're going to get back on your feet and get a new start on life. In the meantime, consider this a blessing. We all need a little help sometimes, in one form or another."

"Right now, we can use all the help we can get."

"By the way, why don't you and Naomi visit our church sometime? In fact, I'd be glad to have you in my Sunday school class for young couples."

"Maybe we'll do that," Ben replied as they got up to leave. "Thanks for your help."

◑ ◑ ◑

"Mr. and Mrs. Wister, your petition for bankruptcy protection in accordance with Chapter 13 of the Federal Bankruptcy Code is approved," Judge Martinez said. "There are conditions associated with this action, and one of them is that you must remain current on the repayment plan established by this court. Do you understand this clearly?"

"Yes, ma'am, we do," replied Ben.

"The bankruptcy court is provided to give people who have had personal financial setbacks beyond their control the chance to start over again.

"I hope you have learned from your bad experiences with the overuse of credit and that you will not repeat the same mistakes. You're young and can reestablish your lives and your credit if you discipline yourselves."

Naomi sat in stunned silence as she came to grips with the reality of her situation. She felt horrible that the judge was chastening them in public for their overuse of credit. She was nearly in tears with shame as the courtroom cleared and just wanted to go home where she could weep in privacy.

"What's the matter?" Ben asked as he and the attorney approached her.

"I'm so embarrassed by this. We never should have charged so much. Our creditors must think we're awful people."

"Everyone makes mistakes," Joe said. "It's good that you recognize your past faults, but you can't afford to dwell on them. The past is history, and starting today you need to concentrate on building a better future. Your debt payments are going to be manageable, and you'll be on solid ground within five years."

"The problem is, this never would have happened to my mom and dad," Naomi said. "They never got in over their heads, and they always paid their bills on time. I should have known better. We borrowed all that money in good faith, and now we're not going to pay it all back."

"That may be true, but remember—you'll have a child to raise, and that child's future will be much more secure as a result of what happened here today."

"Yes," Naomi replied. "But . . ."

Ben broke in. "I agree with Joe. And I'll say it again: I think this bankruptcy is an answer from God."

"Of course," responded Joe. "Even God provided a way to set aside debts so that His people wouldn't be caught up in debts they couldn't repay."

"What do you mean?" Naomi asked.

"In the Old Testament God had a plan: every seven years all debts would be set aside. That's where our bankruptcy laws originated."

"I never heard anybody explain that before," Ben said. "So God allows for bankruptcy too?"

"Absolutely," replied Joe. "Otherwise I wouldn't be in this business."

As Ben and Naomi headed home she commented, "Ben, I'm still embarrassed about this bankruptcy, and I feel like we're cheating our creditors."

"I don't," Ben replied. "It feels like a burden has been lifted off our shoulders. We have a chance to start fresh and get our lives back in order, and pay back in a way that's doable. Wait and see; things are going to work out from now on."

Months later, Naomi began to believe that Ben was right. The pressures on their marriage eased as a result of the bankruptcy, which lessened the financial strain from their delinquent bills. In addition, Ben was able to work extra overtime as his company increased its productivity. They were thrilled with their baby son, Timmy, and they used the extra income from Ben's overtime to buy baby supplies and the other items they needed.

Naomi's mind was so occupied with caring for Timmy that she rarely thought of the bankruptcy. Her mother stayed and helped her until the baby was nearly a month old before returning to her own home.

On her own without her mom's help, Naomi's stress level was higher, but it was still manageable. Unfortunately, Ben pushed Naomi's stress level over the limit when he again became lax in taking care of the household bills. In addition, he began to pick up food in the evenings rather than eat at home.

"There just doesn't seem to be enough money each month," Ben complained. "There was for a while, but it seems to evaporate. We just can't make it on my salary, Naomi. Most couples we know have to have two incomes. That's reality."

"But who would take care of Timmy if I went back to work?" Naomi asked as the tears began to flow. She felt like she was in a dark pit with the sides beginning to cave in.

"Maybe we can get your mom to, at least for a while, until we can get some of the bills caught up," Ben said.

"I hate doing that," Naomi replied. "We're always having to ask for someone's help."

Naomi did go back to work and found that she actually enjoyed it. Although she missed Timmy, being away from him during the day helped her to cope with being up with him at night.

But after a few weeks, her mother told her that, much as she loved and enjoyed her grandson, she could no longer take care of him every day. Naomi fretted over the decision, but in the end she knew her mother was right, so she started looking for someone else. She was shocked at the cost of childcare. She finally selected what she thought would be the best childcare center, but it would cost them a good chunk of money each week.

As the weeks passed, she and Ben continued to argue about money. Naomi believed she was a slave to Ben's impulses. He often bought things he wanted, such as a new television or a better CD player, but then there was no money for needed clothes or to treat themselves to eating out. And he often took money from the ATM but failed to deduct the amount from the checkbook. Finally, she decided that she would keep a portion of her paycheck for herself. Instead of bringing the check home as she had in the past, she would stop at the bank and deposit it, taking out the money she needed.

Ben was furious when she told him about it. "Naomi, you can't do that," he argued. "There won't be enough money to pay all the bills."

"Then they will have to go unpaid," Naomi retorted. "I'm not going to worry about it anymore. You never paid my dad back for his loan, and I'm going to start paying him back something every month. Ben, you act like an irresponsible child. I'm sick and tired of working all day and never being able to spend any of my own money."

"Well, if it's your money, why don't you just keep it yourself, and I'll keep my money!" Ben shouted as he stormed out of the room.

"Fine!" Naomi shouted back as he slammed the door.

Naomi spent the next two hours drawing up a budget, dividing their respective expenses. She decided that she should pay for the baby's childcare, her transportation, and a fourth of the utilities.

The next day she left work a little early so that she could go to the bank and open a checking account in her name. That evening she informed Ben that she had decided to keep her money and pay her own bills. She handed him a copy of the division of expenses that she had drawn up.

Ben had a sinking feeling inside, as if something was dying. And in truth he knew that something was: their marriage.

"Look, Naomi, I'm sorry for what I said last night. I didn't mean it. I don't want us to have separate checking accounts and split the expenses."

"No, you just want to be able to spend what you want, when you want," Naomi fired back. "Well, no more. You pay your part, and I'll pay my part from now on. And if you don't like it, I'll take Timmy and leave."

"Do you really mean that?" Ben asked, hurt.

"I really do," she replied defiantly. "I don't even know if I love you anymore, but I do know that I don't respect you. I've been on the giving end of our marriage from the first day. From now on I'm going to do what's best for me."

Ben felt as if someone had just hit him in the stomach with a sledgehammer. *How did everything go wrong?* he thought as Naomi flounced out of the dining room. *How could I have been stupid enough to let our relationship disintegrate? I don't know what to do now.* For the first time in a long time Ben fell to his knees and asked God to forgive him and help him to heal his marriage.

❍ ❍ ❍

Ben and Naomi represent many couples today, Christian and non-Christian alike. They enter marriage with little or no understanding of finances and quickly find themselves overwhelmed by the opportunities they encounter to spend more than they make. Since opposites do attract, usually one partner is an optimist, who generally looks toward the future to straighten out any errors in the present. The other, a worrier, needs stability and security.

Optimists don't purposely lie to their spouses. They convince themselves that things will change for the better. Ben was an optimist. Naomi, the worrier, became suspicious of Ben because of what appeared to be deceptions and financial irresponsibility. She was forced to drop out of school and give up her career plans, for which she blamed Ben. Then the additional pressure of an unexpected infant added to their financial problems.

After coaching a multitude of couples of all ages in circumstances nearly identical to Ben and Naomi's, I think I can say with some degree of certainty that the financial situation in which they found themselves was indicative of their lack of training and knowledge. They were not stupid—just ignorant. "A prudent man sees danger and takes refuge, but the simple keep going and suffer for it" (Proverbs 22:3).

Ben was living in a dream world and angering his wife as he did so. He refused to take responsibility for his decisions and tried to blame their problems on Naomi. If she went to work, he reasoned, their problems would be solved. If she had taken her birth control pills, she wouldn't have gotten pregnant. God directed the husband to protect and comfort his wife, but Ben tried to shift the blame to her and sneak around behind her back with his personal indulgences.

<blockquote>
CHAPTER
</blockquote>

BUD and SANDI:
WHERE *Indulgence* LEADS

Bud and Sandi Hawkins were Christians. Bud was a stockbroker and made an average annual salary that kept them very comfortable. He took care of the mortgage payments, car payments and insurance, utilities, the children's private school tuition, and his and Sandi's college loans. He figured out how much food, gasoline, clothing, and other household necessities should cost and gave Sandi that amount to manage.

Their marriage was a good one, except in the area of finances. Sandi sensed that she was not a part of any major financial decisions in either their personal lives or the business where Bud was a participating partner. With their children in school during the day, Sandi would liked to have worked part-time in Bud's office, as she had when he first started. However, the other members of the firm had established policies that prohibited the involvement of family members in the business. So Sandi kept busy with the children's activities and volunteer work through their church.

Bud seemed to have a knack for selling securities. He understood the business and his clients were happy with the job he did in helping them find solid, well-performing companies to invest in. But over time, Bud began turning his attention to land development. Real estate was booming, and he figured he could make a lot more money—and make it faster.

Against Sandi's counsel, he borrowed sizable amounts of money from a local bank and invested it in what seemed to her to be risky real estate ventures. He even took on potential liabilities as a managing partner in several investments with others in the firm—again over his wife's vehement objections. With dollar signs in his eyes, Bud simply dismissed her concerns. Sandi felt like she had been relegated to the position of a child instead of an adult partner in the family's financial matters, and she resented it.

Things went fine for a while. Then one of the land investments in which Bud was a managing partner went sour. Everyone involved lost a great deal of money. One major investor accused Bud of mismanagement and filed a lawsuit against him. The suit called for the return of the money the investor had entrusted to Bud.

"You brought this on yourself," Sandi said as she looked at a copy of the lawsuit.

"Please, not now, Sandi," Bud pleaded, as he lowered his head into his hands. "I'm feeling really beaten down right now. I guess you don't understand."

"Sure, I understand. Your good friends have decided to let you hold the bag for the entire firm," Sandi said with an accusing tone. "I told you not to do business with Jerry Groves. There was something about him I didn't like the first time I met him."

"Oh, spare me the sermon," Bud growled. "This has to be the 999th time you've said that. It's always, 'You never take my advice,' and 'You never listen to me.' Sandi, this is serious. Don't you realize how much trouble this can cause me?"

"Can cause *us*, Bud. How much trouble it can cause *us*. That's our main trouble now: You think you're in it alone if it is a financial decision."

"Hey, just what is it you expect from me?" he countered. "I work hard, and I've tried my best to provide a good home for you and the kids."

"True. You have," she replied in a softer tone. "But I don't really care about material things. I just want us to talk about these things and agree, but you treat me like I'm some kind of an idiot when it comes to finances. You listen to everyone else's advice but not mine."

I wish I could really be honest with her, Bud thought. *If I could just once share how I feel without her saying, "I told you so."*

"Bud, when will you finally admit that you don't really want my help?" Sandi said as he started to leave the room. "But maybe this time you've gotten yourself in deep enough to admit that you actually need me."

During the following months Bud's situation grew worse. The disgruntled investor continued to pursue the lawsuit. And Bud continued to hide most of the facts from Sandi, believing that he was sparing her the emotional trauma he was experiencing. Then one day Sandi read in the local newspaper that all of their property and possessions were listed for possible auction by the district court, pending an upcoming assessment for investment fraud against Bud.

When Bud came home that evening, Sandi vented the frustration she had been feeling for years. Not that their marriage was all bad—in many ways they had a better marriage than most, and they had shared many pleasant times together. But Sandi had always felt like an observer in their finances, instead of a partner.

"You told me that lawsuit would amount to nothing," she shouted, "and now I find out from reading the paper that we have a judgment against us! Is that what you call nothing?"

"I'm sorry, Sandi. I wanted to tell you weeks ago that the judge had decided against us, but I just didn't know how."

"I thought you told me there was nothing to that suit. How could you have lost?"

"I don't know," Bud said. "They even offered to settle when the case began, but my attorney didn't want to because he felt the facts were so obviously in our favor." The dejected look on his face spoke volumes.

"So exactly what does it mean that you lost?" Sandi asked, as fear began to well up inside of her.

"It means that we have to file for bankruptcy, or they'll take our home and everything else. I know I've done a lot of foolish things. I'm sorry I didn't listen to you or let you be a part of the decisions."

"I have to be honest, Bud," Sandi said with tears in her eyes. "I'm really scared, but I don't think we should file for bankruptcy. Maybe the Lord won't rescue us from the mess we're in, but if we don't give Him the chance we'll always wonder what He would have done."

"But it could mean we'll end up totally broke. After ten years of marriage we should have something more to show for it."

"I don't care about that stuff. You and I were closer when we had nothing than we are now. I've been praying that we could get back to that. Maybe this is the Lord's way of answering," Sandi said as she walked over to her husband and put her arms around him.

❍ ❍ ❍

Indulgence, impulse buying, and get-rich-quick schemes all have the same root cause: greed. Most of us don't like to hear that, because we're all prone to at least one of those problems. In reality, they are just different levels of the same basic problem. Bud suffered from a get-rich-quick mentality that manifested itself in his taking excessive investment risks. God brought a balancer into his life—his wife Sandi—but he excluded her from decisions involving money.

Bud indulged himself through his investments, just as another person might through the purchase of expensive cars, houses, or jewelry. Each of us has special indulgences that stem from an attitude of lust. Lust is not limited to the area of sex. In our society, people may lust more after power and wealth than after sex.

Often we have the mistaken idea that more money will solve our financial problems. Bud—and others like him—is living proof that more money can easily result in bigger problems. Men who invest in high-risk deals that fail often transfer the blame to other people. Since the family is the most readily available scapegoat, they are the ones who usually receive the blame. "I was doing it to better provide for my family," the man says. Nonsense. He did it because it fed his ego and was a chance to get rich quickly.

JACKSON and LINN:
EXPECT *the* UNEXPECTED

Jackson and Linn came from different economic backgrounds.

Linn's mother was a stay-at-home mom, but that hardly describes her energy and passion. She volunteered in the children's wing at the local hospital twice a week, reading stories, preparing crafts, and engaging the children in activities to keep their minds and their restless bodies occupied as much as possible. When Linn was old enough, she sometimes accompanied her mother.

In the church Linn's mother was the go-to woman for anything regarding Sunday school, vacation Bible school, and curriculum for kids' and youth clubs. She called Linn her "right-hand girl" and allowed her to help in small ways from the time she was very young. As she grew older, Linn was able to be a true assistant, and began teaching her own Sunday school class when she was in high school. She discovered she was gifted in this area and determined to go to college and pursue a teaching career. And, if she happened to marry someone and have her own children someday, she would stay at home while they were young, and then, when they were in school, she could return to teaching, so her schedule would coincide with theirs, and the family would be home together.

Linn's father was a successful businessman, and although he was not wealthy, he made a very comfortable living. He was also involved in the church and in community organizations, believing that to whom much was given, much was expected. Though a friendly man, he was more comfortable with administrative roles than the people-involved tasks his wife and daughter loved.

Linn was not indulged as a child, and she was expected to work to help pay her way from the time she was a teenager. Her college tuition was provided by her parents, but she was required to work summers to earn money for her books, clothes, and incidentals, which she did.

Jackson came from a much more modest background. His mother and father, both from broken homes themselves, were divorced when he was nine years old. He missed his father in the home and grew to resent being away from his friends on weekends to visit him at the apartment he now lived in. His parents both expressed their grievances against each other to him, and by the time Jackson was a teenager, he had decided he'd never get married, never wanting to put another child through the pain of a broken family.

His mother struggled financially after the divorce, and money was always in short supply in his home. As soon as he was old enough, he found jobs that provided him with spending money and enabled him to help his mother with living expenses.

Jackson's pastor helped him apply for a scholarship from his denomination to attend a Bible college. Part of the condition of the award money was that he would teach in a Christian school for at least two years, which suited Jackson fine. One of his junior high teachers had taken an interest in him and helped him through those difficult years, and Jackson later decided that he would also like to be a teacher and help kids. He worked long hours to pay his expenses during his Bible college years.

After graduation, Jackson accepted a teaching position as a junior high math teacher in a small Christian school. Sticking to his resolve to remain unmarried, he seemed oblivious to the attempts by others on the school staff and in his church to match him up with the right young woman. He was content as he was.

During the summer after his second year of teaching, the school hired a new teacher to take the split fifth/sixth grade class. It was Linn. She and Jackson quickly got acquainted, and, while it wasn't exactly love at first sight, Jackson suspected his self-imposed bachelor days were coming to an end. He and Linn were married in a simple ceremony during spring break that year, with their school community, church friends, and parents in attendance. They decided to hold off having children indefinitely. Jackson was still a little skittish about bringing a child into the world, and Linn wanted to have several terms of teaching under her belt before taking a few years off to be home with children. Besides, they wanted to have a nest egg of savings on hand.

But, as everyone eventually learns, life rarely follows a predictable course. When they had been married just two years, they learned that Linn was pregnant.

Despite his misgivings, Jackson found himself excited. He and Linn were in a committed, Christ-centered marriage, and he knew they would break his family's tendency toward broken relationships. And Linn had always planned on being a mother, so she was also pleased, though a little worried at the prospect of their losing her financial contribution. The school they worked for paid low salaries, and they had been unable to accumulate any significant savings. But they were able to live frugally, and they did have what seemed to be an adequate insurance plan, so they thought they would be all right financially. The baby would be born during their summer break, so Linn would be able to work right up to the time of the birth. They decided to forgo an ultrasound that would tell them what the baby's gender was, preferring to be surprised. The pregnancy was going so smoothly that they thought maybe they'd have their second child sooner than later.

There were two things that they hadn't planned on. One was that Jackson's salary alone was too low to meet their minimum needs, regardless of how much they scrimped, and two was that the baby would have major health problems. Jordan was born with a form of spina bifida and required constant attention. The initial hospital bill was more than $82,000, with their deductible portion being almost $30,000.

Within six months of the baby's birth, they were in debt for nearly $55,000 and sinking further behind every month. When they attempted to pay any portion of the doctor or hospital bills, they fell behind on payments for their monthly living expenses. If they tried to keep up on their living expenses, they fell behind on their medical bills.

By the seventh month some of the accounts had been turned over to collection agencies, and Linn was getting frequent, often rude calls at home. She was worn out, and saw her dreams of having a second child and maybe a third and then returning to teaching vanishing before her eyes. They couldn't make it with one, and his needs prevented her from even thinking about going back to work. Their pediatrician—a friend from church—suggested that they consider filing bankruptcy to relieve some of the financial pressure.

Coming home from the doctor's office Linn asked, "What did you think about what Doctor Yuan said?"

"I don't know. I've always believed that you should pay your bills, but that seems to be impossible in our case. Every month we get further behind. What do you think?"

"I don't know the answer either. But I do know I can't live under the kind of pressure I feel right now. We can't pay the doctor or hospital bills anyway, so I don't see what difference it would make if we file for bankruptcy. If we're ever able to pay, we can always start repaying the bills, can't we?"

"I guess so," Jackson replied. "I don't feel at peace about it, but I honestly don't know of another alternative. I'll call an attorney I know from the men's group and ask if he handles cases like these or can recommend someone.

But we don't even have the money to pay a lawyer unless he or she would agree to take his fee in installments."

Though they loved Jordan dearly and would do anything for his benefit, the glow had gone from their lives and the future looked bleak.

BETH:
The IMPORTANCE *of* THINKING AHEAD

When Beth Kramer's father died suddenly of a heart attack, she was ten, her sister was fourteen, and their mother, who had gone from her parents' home to marriage, had no idea how to manage the household accounts.

Fortunately, the house was nearly paid for and the family car still had some life in it. But Mrs. Kramer had been raised with the assumption that she would become a wife and mother, so she had not gone to college or acquired any other training and had no job experience to fall back on. Her late husband's small pension would take care of the house payment, but not much else.

Beth and her sister had known the comforts of middle-class living. Both girls had received allowances that were sufficient for them to enjoy the same pleasures their friends and classmates had, and though their lifestyle was modest, they never wanted for anything and never felt that their friends had more than they did. The family took a vacation every year, traveling from their home in Pennsylvania to visit family in Indiana, and had once gone to Disney World.

Mrs. Kramer had a good sense of fashion and instilled in her daughters the importance of looking well for every occasion. She enjoyed sewing, and would make her girls stylish outfits for holidays and special events.

When Mr. Kramer died, the church was supportive, bringing casseroles for two weeks and offering help: "Please let me know if there's anything I can do." The people were sincere, but Mrs. Kramer knew it was up to her to support herself and her two children.

She went to a neighborhood dry cleaners that advertised alterations, but they were not hiring. However, they said they could use her services on an as-needed basis for minor alterations, replacing zippers, and other such work. But while this brought in a little cash, it was by far too little and too irregular to pay bills.

Beth's mother was an intelligent woman, but she and her husband had never discussed finances. She was responsible for the home, and her husband was responsible for the checkbook and household management. Two months after his death she was receiving past due notices and threats to cut off utilities because she hadn't paid the bills.

She went to the bank and confided to a manager her need to understand how to handle a checkbook. He was kind, and took her to his office. He produced a sample checkbook, opened it to the first check, and explained, "This is check number one." Mrs. Kramer told Beth years later, "I can still feel my face burning with embarrassment." The banker went on to show her how to record deposits, subtract check amounts, and reconcile her statement every month. She soon became quite good at managing.

After a few months, Mrs. Kramer went to her pastor and explained her need to earn a living to see if he had any ideas. Pastor McCoy worked with her to determine what experiences and abilities she had, and finally suggested she use her homemaking talents to open a catering business. She was agreeable, and the pastor made contacts with people he knew in several churches in town, recommending her services.

With the girls' help and later a part-time assistant, she was able to get her business off the ground. Beth and her sister found themselves going from having fun family times and stylish made-to-order outfits to wearing clothes from the thrift store and clearance racks, and spending vacation time and special days cooking and serving others for *their* special events.

The family struggled, and there never seemed to be quite enough money. Beth felt they were now different from "other families." "Other families" went on vacation. "In other families, the kids don't have to help their mother cook." And to their dismay, the houses in their area were reassessed, and the property taxes suddenly skyrocketed. Mrs. Kramer felt she could no longer afford the house, so she put it up for sale, and the family moved to an apartment. Beth couldn't help thinking, "Other families live in houses."

Because she didn't want her girls to bear her burdens, Mrs. Kramer kept the state of the family finances to herself. Beth and Nancy were provided for, but Beth always felt like there was never enough, and that she couldn't ask for or expect extras. Though she meant well, Mrs. Kramer, in her desire to keep the girls from worry, never taught them how to handle money.

Having a career in catering meant Mrs. Kramer could arrange her schedule to spend time with her girls, and the modest business made it possible to get by through Beth's senior year of high school. After that, she found a job at a big-box store, a position with benefits that paid well enough and even offered a retirement plan. Beth's older sister, Nancy, had gone to college for nursing on state grants and student loans, and was now happily working in a hospital in western Pennsylvania.

Beth lived at home for two years while attending community college. She knew she didn't want to go into debt for an education, so she worked at a home improvement store and paid for her classes herself. She only took a few classes at a time, though, because she was unwilling to spend all of her money, and anyway, she didn't know what kind of classes to take or what sort of career she should prepare for. She started a savings account and added to it every payday. Soon she had a thousand dollars of her own. She was determined to never again know what it was like to have to make do with the clothes she already owned and never treat herself to something new, or to have to decline going to a restaurant or a movie with friends because she had no money in her pocket.

After two years, Nancy invited Beth to live with her and share expenses. Beth was ready to leave home, so, with her mother's blessing, she moved a few hours away to join her sister. She had grown interested in graphic arts by that time and found a good program near her new home.

She decided to use her savings to begin the semester and pay her share of the rent, and soon her account had dwindled. She found a part-time job on campus and quickly became absorbed in her studies. She attended church with Nancy and there made friends. After a year, Nancy got married, and Beth moved into another apartment with two young women she had met at church.

The new apartment was unfurnished, so the three went shopping. Beth used her credit card for her share of the purchases and hit her limit before she knew it. She accepted an offer for another credit card and then another.

Before the second year of schooling, Beth applied for and received student loans. Her part-time job was sufficient to pay rent, and she was able to pay the minimum amounts due on all three of her credit cards. She enjoyed being single and independent, and was able to charge new clothes and go out socially with friends and not feel that she had to deny herself. Once in a while she would be concerned at the high balances on her credit card statements, but as long as she was paying the minimum due, she put the worries out of her mind.

After she graduated, Beth found a job in her field and moved into her own apartment. She made enough in salary to afford a down payment on a new car. Her rent was higher, she now had car payments, and her student loans were coming due. But she was able to meet her basic payments with her paycheck, and took care of the rest, such as gas and sometimes groceries, with credit. Her savings were long gone, and she had no extra money to put anything away anyway. She was active in her church, but felt it would be more responsible to pay her bills instead of giving to church. When the offering plate came by, she became quite good at stuffing a small bill in her hand and tucking it into a plate so no one would notice she never gave with a check or used an envelope.

For a while she tried to pay down her credit cards by paying five dollars over the minimum, but the balance never seemed to change. Her credit, however, was good, since she was making at least minimum payments. Once or twice when her checking account was nearly empty several days before payday, she took a cash advance from a credit card and deposited it in her checking account. And often when she went out with friends she would offer to "make things easier" by charging the meal on her card and collecting cash from her friends, thereby tiding her over to the next payday.

But then her old washer gave out for good. It was not worth repairing again. This happened the week she had finally acknowledged that her car's bald tires needed to be replaced, which she paid for with the money that should have gone to her cell phone bill. She had been used to juggling monthly bills for years, but never was able to catch up. Paying a double cell phone bill one month meant she had to skip the cable bill, so that had to be doubled the next month. She was habitually a month late on her car payment. She even began to fall behind on her credit card payments, leaving her with no credit to use to buy a new washer. Beth didn't know anyone else in her circle of friends who was forced to go to a Laundromat. She was embarrassed to be in her midthirties and outwardly successful in her career, but with only a drawer full of bills to show for it. She was in so much debt she told herself she'd still be working to pay it all off when she was eighty. She was generally happy with her life, had a close circle of friends, a wide range of interests and activities, and was content to be single, but she knew it was up to her to take care of her own finances.

Around that time, several churches in their town got together and invited a financial expert to talk about the Bible's teaching on money. Beth attended, and was surprised to learn that the Bible said so much about money and its management. She took the expert's advice on setting up a budget and actually did better for about a year. She nearly stopped charging and tried, with some success, to stay within her budget. However, there was no personal accountability, and she soon fell back into her old habits.

Then she was involved in a minor traffic accident. Though no one was hurt, the repairs were costly, and she had to use her rent money to pay the five hundred dollar deductible. She then had to put off her cell phone and a couple of utility bills to pay the rent, putting her behind for a couple of months. Without savings to fall back on and with her credit cards maxed out, she grew panicky that she was in a hole she'd never get out of.

By now Beth understood that her reluctance to deny herself materially was a result of her family's struggles after her father's death. She hadn't liked having to do without when she perceived that her friends could have anything they wanted. She hadn't liked feeling different. As an adult, she enjoyed supporting herself and being successful in her career, but she carried that determination to enjoy things money could buy with her, and her lack of self-control had gotten her into trouble. Now she was tired of living with anxiety—not from fear of not having things as nice as her friends, but real fear of never getting out of the cycle of debt.

CHAPTER

PENNY:
HOW EASY *It* IS

Penny Balosek came from a hardworking family that "made good."

Her grandparents had emigrated from Europe, proud to become Americans while retaining strong ethnic roots. Her grandfather started in a steel mill as a batch/melter, and eventually became a rolling machine operator. He provided a good home for his wife and several children and spoke English well, though his speech never discarded its eastern European flavor.

Penny's father, Rudy, carried on the family heritage of working hard, and he also worked for a few years in the mill. But his goal was to have a job where he would wear a suit for work and return to his home cool and sharp. At the age of twenty-two he left the mill and took a job as a waiter in the restaurant of an upscale hotel. Within two years he was the maitre d', and a year after that he had moved on to manage a high-end steak house downtown.

Rudy Balosek learned as much as he needed to in the next five years, and when he was thirty, got married, moved to the suburbs, and opened a family restaurant he simply called Rudolf's. Over the years, he opened Rudolf's East and Rudolf's West, earning good reviews when his businesses were rated in the city newspapers. He opened Rudy's Bar & Grill when his oldest son finished college with a business degree and made him a partner as a graduation gift.

Rudy's second son was not interested in being a business owner, but he made a good living in medical supplies.

Penny came along several years after her brothers. Her life was busy with school, friends, a large extended family, and social activities with their Orthodox church. Each summer through her sophomore year of high school, she spent two weeks at a camp for children and youth of her ethnic upbringing, where they learned of their heritage, practiced dances, had conversational language lessons, and cooked.

Penny's parents did not expect her to attend college. They assumed she'd settle down with a boy from the church and happily create a new generation for the Balosek family tree. But after she and David had been dating for three years, they decided not to get married, to the disappointment of both families. Tired of her job in the grocery store, Penny took a course in data management through a technical school and went to work for a dental practice owned by a distant relative.

When she was twenty, she moved out of her parents' home into a townhouse. Her parents gifted her with a down payment, believing it was wasteful to pay rent when she was able to invest in a property. She was excelling at her job and found she enjoyed it. Her take-home pay was plenty to cover the house payment, insurance, utilities, and even the expense of the new, heavily financed car she had chosen with her father's help.

She went shopping with her mother to furnish her new place. Penny had always paid off both of her credit cards in full each month, so she had plenty of available credit. She and her mother found reasonably priced but high-quality pieces to fill the living room and bedroom, and then purchased appliances and a large-screen TV. Penny wavered a bit when she figured up the total she had put on her card in just one day, but what else could she have done? She couldn't sit on crates. She took a day off work to wait for the delivery of her things, and since that all occurred in the morning, spent the afternoon charging her purchases for art and colored pillows and the like to splash her townhouse with her own sense of style.

She had been used to having her necessities paid for and actually made a conscious decision not to lower her standard of living. *What for?* she reasoned. She had a good job, was only responsible for herself, and liked nice things. She didn't bother renting DVDs; instead she bought her favorites. She dressed well for work, purposely dressing in suits, since she was a professional in the business office of the dental practice, and didn't need to wear scrubs as the hygienists and assistants did. She opened charge accounts in several classy department stores. She enjoyed vacations with friends or some of her many cousins, financing it all with plastic. Penny didn't concern herself with the total amount of debt she was accumulating, since she had no trouble making the minimum payments. She added another major credit card to her wallet, and her original two increased her spending limit.

Penny often shifted balances around to other cards to take advantage of better offers and interest rates, and thereby prided herself on handling her money well. By the time she was thirty, Penny had accumulated $20,000 in consumer debt.

Around that time, she decided to move on from the dental practice and found a job with a large insurance company in the city. Her commute was longer, but her car was still running well and was nearly paid for. She was startled, however, when, during her initial interview, the rep from human resources told her that employees were encouraged to keep their personal finances in order because major credit problems could hinder their performance. Penny decided to rein in her spending and within two years was able to cut her debt in half.

But then her car gave out, and she decided to again finance a new one rather than saving for a used one, telling herself there was no point in inheriting someone else's problems. Her payments were still affordable, though she had very little spendable income after all the bills were paid. She quickly found herself $15,000 dollars in debt.

One of Penny's friends at her new job was Suzanne Duncan, who was about the same age. Suzanne was enthusiastic about a financial seminar she'd heard about, and invited Penny to come to a free introductory session. The speaker was Thom Handleman, and he repeated a catchy if corny slogan about handling your money instead of the other way around. He was a mesmerizing and motivating speaker, and Penny began to take notes, but soon contented herself with listening. She was enamored with his ideas on how to make her money work for her rather than feel enslaved by the constant cycle of need-want-charge-worry.

When she got home, she tried to remember all Thom Handleman had taught, but could only remember her enthusiasm and not what she had been so enthused about. So she signed up for his day-long seminar, which was only five hundred dollars and included a boxed lunch, a DVD of the session she was about to attend, an excerpt from one of his bestselling books, a binder filled with "Handle Your Money!" resources and products, and seven hours in the presence of the financial expert.

After the seminar, Penny didn't feel she was ready to take Handleman's advice on investing in real estate, but she liked his idea of purchasing silver bullion. He had spent an entire hour of the morning session raving about the future of silver—how it had multiple industrial uses because of its malleability and ductility (she reread that part in the resource section several times), and also how it was being used more and more in hospital burn units to prevent bacterial infections. She read that many wound care products incorporate a layer of fabric that contains silver. Handleman pointed out that anyone with a social conscience should want to invest in such a commodity.

So Penny took out a cash advance of $5,000 on a credit card and purchased silver bullion. She was excited about it when it was delivered and kept it in her safe box at the bank. She was not clear how a chunk of silver in a bank box helped burn victims, but Handleman's method directed that she would resell when the market for silver went up, as it was sure to, and that her profit would enable her to turn around and invest in other worthy commodities.

Penny hadn't spent her entire cash advance on silver. She meant to pay the remaining amount right back into her card, but never quite got around to it. She left it in her checking account and, when it was gone, couldn't fully account for its disappearance. Well, she had upgraded the sound system in her car to make the commute more comfortable . . . and she had nearly paid off one of her smaller department store cards. Telling herself she was choosing wisely, she had taken advantage of a big-box store's computer sale and selected just the laptop she needed. She had treated herself to a lavish "girls' getaway spa package" for a weekend with some friends from church . . . Yes, she was sure all that money hadn't been wasted. And of course there was the bullion in her safe box.

One weekend, when Penny was unexpectedly home on a Saturday evening, she decided to try out the budgeting software she had purchased around the time she had started her new job, but that she had never installed. As she went through her accounts, she was appalled to see laid out right on her computer screen how much she owed in comparison to what she was making monthly. Somehow it had never dawned on her that she was spending far more than she brought in, or else had never allowed the realization to take root.

Penny searched for "debt reduction," entered her zip code, found several companies that offered services, and chose the one whose name seemed the most interesting. She e-mailed for an appointment.

PART TWO:

...AND HOW THEY CLIMBED OUT

CHAPTER 6

BEN *and* NAOMI REVISITED

How did Ben and Naomi Wister get out of debt? It took hard work and a commitment to follow scriptural principles concerning the handling of money.

Ben realized that he had placed his marriage in great jeopardy and that Naomi was thinking of calling it quits.

Several times in the past Naomi had asked Ben to call her pastor and set up an appointment for counseling, but Ben had always refused, saying that he knew more about handling money than the average pastor. And he always had the promise of more income just around the corner that would solve their problems. But after Naomi opened her own checking account, it was Ben who asked her if she would go to the pastor with him. She flatly refused.

No pastor is going to be able to help our marriage, Naomi thought as she drove out of the driveway one morning, not long after she had set up the new bank account in her name. *I don't know if anything's left. Do I still love Ben?* she wondered. *I don't know. Our whole married life has been one continual struggle over money.*

All day she thought about her options and silently prayed. As far as she was concerned, her marriage was over—and she didn't know what she was going to do. She had purposely opened her own checking account so that she could accumulate some funds if, and when, she went out on her own. But she knew she didn't make enough money to pay for childcare, a place to live, a car, and other expenses. She was shocked by her own thoughts. Had she actually been planning to leave Ben? Then she realized that it was not a divorce she wanted. She wanted to be free of the pressures they had been facing since the day they got married. Ben was a good man, and she believed he loved her. It was just that he was so irresponsible about money.

That evening Naomi found Ben already home and preparing supper in the kitchen. "Ben," she said in genuine astonishment, "why are you home so early? Is anything wrong at work?"

"No," Ben said without looking up. "I just realized that because of my stupidity I have lost something very precious to me." He pulled her to himself and hugged her, as Timmy played happily on the floor. "It's not more money I need. I need help. I called Pastor Rhimer today and explained what a mess I've made of our finances and our marriage. The pastor is willing to work with me on the marriage, but he recommended a financial coach in the church to help with our finances. So I called him."

"Ben, I think that's great," Naomi said with enthusiasm.

"But the financial coach won't meet unless we both go. I didn't know what to tell him," Ben said.

Naomi knew what he wanted her to say.

"Call and tell him we'll be glad to meet," Naomi said as she rested in his arms. "I just pray there is a way out of the mess we're in."

Ben and Naomi met with the coach, Bryan Stanford, the following week. Bryan asked them each to complete a short personality test before the session actually began. A few minutes later he called them into his office.

"Come in," he said in a friendly tone. "Take a seat. Before we begin, let's pray."

As Bryan was asking the Lord to give them wisdom in their time together, Ben realized that it had been months since he had even felt the desire to pray or read the Bible, although both had been habits for most of his life. The pressures they were under seemed to have stripped him of his ability to concentrate. He realized the same must have been true for Naomi.

When he finished praying, Bryan said, "Ben, tell me what you think the problems are."

Ben was surprised by the question, because he had expected that a financial coach would ask to see the multitude of records they had brought with them. "I honestly don't know. I suppose it has to be my handling of the money. We never seem to have enough to pay all the bills. We still owe Naomi's dad for most of the loan he made so we could catch up. We owe for two cars, a consolidation loan with the credit union, and our house. And the repayment plan from the bankruptcy."

"Thanks, Ben," he said.

Then turning to Naomi, Bryan asked, "What do you think the problem is?"

"Well, I guess it's much like Ben said, except that I believe the real problem—at least in our marriage—is that we don't discuss things. We argue, and I see it getting worse instead of better."

"Are you willing to make the changes necessary to cure the problems, rather than just treat the symptoms?" Bryan asked them both.

"I'm ready to do whatever I have to do," Ben said.

"I think I am too," agreed Naomi.

"Good," Bryan replied. "Especially since I believe God put you two together to operate as a team. I generally find that when a husband and wife work together, they each bring a needed perspective to the finances. But the specific problems must be dealt with first. Then we'll decide who should do what.

"I need to get an idea about where you are financially right now, so I'm going to ask you some questions, Ben. Feel free to speak up, Naomi, if you think Ben has missed anything or you have some input."

Bryan took out one of his budget worksheets and started down the list of monthly expenses. Ben gave most of the answers, but when it came to regular expenses, such as those for clothes, food, laundry, and childcare, he deferred to Naomi's better memory.

When they had completed the list, the coach began to list their outstanding debts. Once they had gone through the obvious debts—the house mortgage, credit union loan, car loans, and family loans—Ben was noticeably hesitant.

"What's the problem, Ben?" Bryan asked, sensing that Ben was holding back.

"I need to tell you something," Ben said hesitantly, "but I'm afraid Naomi will really get upset if I do."

"I can't help you unless I know all the facts," Bryan said. "If you owe something else that's not reflected in our records, you must let me know about it."

"Well, about two months ago, when Naomi and I were having a lot of problems, I bought a new car," Ben confessed.

"You bought a new car!" Naomi exclaimed. "How did you buy a new car? I've never seen it."

"Naomi, give Ben a chance to explain," Bryan cautioned. "He's trying to be honest with you now."

"I bought the car from a local dealer with the understanding that I could return it if Naomi wanted me to. When I got home, that was the day we had a big fight about our Visa account being turned over to a collection agency, remember? So I tried to return the car. That's when I found out that the dealer wanted $650 to take it back."

"Ben, how could you do that without even asking me?" Naomi said angrily.

"Wait a minute, Naomi. Let Ben explain. What's done is done. Let's just try to work this out," Bryan suggested calmly. "Okay?"

"Naomi, I know it was stupid and I should have asked you, but I just got carried away when I stopped to look at the cars. And I honestly thought I could return it. I didn't know they would charge a restocking fee."

"Where does the car loan stand now, Ben?" Bryan asked.

"I signed a note for the $650 so they would take the car back. Now they're threatening to sue me if I don't pay up. But I don't know where the money will come from."

"Okay, a $650 note due and payable," Bryan noted on his worksheet. "Anything else?"

"One thing," Ben replied as he looked over at Naomi and saw her grimace. "I owe five hundred dollars on our Visa for a car navigation system I bought about a month ago."

"I thought you saved the money to buy that from your overtime pay," Naomi said.

"I did, but I decided that I should get the top of the line that had a built-in theft alarm—plus there was an installation fee. It all came to nearly five hundred, and I didn't have the extra money, so I charged the whole thing."

"What happened to the money you had from overtime?" Bryan asked.

"I kept it, planning to use that to pay the Visa bill," Ben replied. "But somehow it all was spent before the bill came."

"So now we owe another five hundred on the Visa?" Naomi looked away as the tears welled up in her eyes.

"Naomi, please calm down," Bryan said in a gentle voice. "We knew the situation was bad, or you wouldn't have come here. But I appreciate Ben's honesty about the debts. I can't be of any help to you if I don't know the entire situation.

"As I see it, you have some pressing debts that have to be dealt with rather quickly. When you elected to file the Chapter 13 bankruptcy, you made an agreement not to incur any additional debts until the payment period expired. Now you have an additional fifteen hundred dollars in debt that the court doesn't know about. The first thing you need to do is deal with that situation. I don't suppose you have any surplus funds that can be used to pay these bills, do you?"

"No, sir," Ben replied. "Only what's in the checking account, which isn't much right now."

"You'll need that for normal living expenses," Bryan said. "Do you have any surplus in your account, Naomi?"

Naomi sat silently for several moments before she spoke. "Yes, I do. But I don't want to use it to pay for Ben's indulgences."

"I can understand that," Bryan said, "but if you're going to work out this situation and find a permanent solution, it will be because you do it together, working as one unit. If you're holding the money as a nest egg in case the marriage doesn't work out, it won't.

"Remember," the coach continued, "Satan would like nothing better than to drive a wedge between you and Ben, and God can only work in your marriage if you make an irrevocable commitment to make it work. God has a role for each of you, and your marriage will work if you follow His principles."

"But Ben doesn't behave responsibly in our home," Naomi protested. "So am I supposed to turn over all the money to him, knowing it will be spent foolishly?"

"No," Bryan assured her. "The way to balance one extreme is not to go to another. God put you two together because you need the balance that each offers the other. You must work together as one. Now is your chance to decide whether you trust God or just *say* that you trust God.

"Anyone can help you manage the money and pay the bills. That's a matter of following a plan I'll outline for you. But the financial problems you have are really symptoms of greater problems that exist. So unless you deal with the root problems, the symptoms will always return. Since the problems are spiritual in nature, only God can cure them.

"No couple can keep their assets separated and be one. Naomi, I can't tell you what to do. All I can do is offer you counsel based on what I believe God would have both you and Ben do. I want you each to take some time to think and pray about your decisions. Call me when you have made a decision, and we'll get back together.

"In the meantime, Ben, I want you to call the bankruptcy court's trustee, George Helms. Give him the facts, and let him know that we're working together. George and I have communicated many times, so if he has a question, tell him to call me. Also, I want you to contact the manager of the bank that holds the note on your car and tell him that we're working out a plan and will be in contact with him in the next two weeks. But you'll have to pay at least the minimum on the Visa bill, or your Chapter 13 plan will be in jeopardy."

During the next few days Naomi hardly spoke to Ben. He tried to be as helpful as possible by doing things around the house and taking Timmy on walks in the evenings.

Naomi found herself in a state of confusion during the week. She had separated herself from Ben financially, if not physically. She considered what Bryan Stanford had said about their problems being as much spiritually based as financially based. Inside she knew he was right. She had been drifting away from the Lord. It was as if her faith had crumbled at the first real test she had ever faced.

Finally, she made the decision to cross the invisible line back into her marriage. She vowed to God that she would commit her resources to her marriage and work at becoming one with Ben. She realized that this might not be the best time in life to finish college, and that she might have to put off her dream of going into marketing, at least for the time being.

Suddenly, having made the decision, she felt free, as if a great burden had been lifted from her shoulders. She could hardly wait to get home.

She arrived home before Ben and was sorting through the mail when she came across an official looking envelope from the Internal Revenue Service. Her stomach did such a flip that she thought she might throw up. She sank down in one of the dining room chairs. She just stared at the envelope for several minutes. She wasn't sure she even wanted to know what it said. She suspected that Ben hadn't filed their taxes properly or that they were being audited.

Finally, she put the envelope down and slid out of the chair to her knees. Resting her elbows on the chair seat, she closed her eyes and began to pray. "Dear God, I know I'm living in fear and dread over our finances. I ask you to forgive my attitude and give me the peace that You promised. I know I have not been following Your path or living by Your plan, but I commit myself to You and to my husband, whatever the circumstances are." She hugged Timmy, who was laughing as he crawled over her.

She stood up and, picking up the envelope, started to open it. *No*, she thought, *I'll wait and let Ben open it. We'll face whatever it is together.* She dropped the letter on the table and began to fix their dinner.

Ben came home a few minutes later and walked over to Naomi. "Hi, honey. How did your day go?" Ben asked cheerfully.

"My day went great," Naomi replied as she wiped her hands and hugged Ben.

Ben was shocked by her sudden display of affection. It had been several months since she had even kissed him voluntarily. Their physical relationship had deteriorated so much that Ben was afraid to show any affection, for fear she would reject him.

"Ben, I know I've been depressed and moody about our finances the last few months," Naomi confessed.

"Don't worry about it," Ben replied. "I've given you plenty of cause to be worried in the past. But I am committed to making a change. I want to be a good husband with God's help."

"Let me say what I want to say first. It doesn't matter about the problems anymore. We'll work them out together as long as you'll let me help. I have decided to close my checking account and put the money into our joint account. I have about five hundred dollars in savings, and I want us to use it to pay off some of the debts."

"Honey, I can't do that," Ben protested. "You earned that money. It seems like somebody else always has to clean up my messes."

"No, you're wrong. The money is not mine," Naomi said emphatically. "It's not really even ours. It belongs to God. We seem to have forgotten that somewhere along the way. I want the money in my account to be used for our expenses."

They just stood there several seconds holding each other. Then Naomi said, "Ben, a letter came from the IRS today. I didn't want to open it, so I left it on the table."

"Oh, no, what now?" Ben said as he picked up the envelope from the table. "I know we don't owe any money to the IRS—at least I don't think we do."

Opening the envelope Ben let out a whoop. "Naomi, we don't owe any money! This is a check for nearly nine hundred dollars!"

"Why did they send us a check?" Naomi asked as she began to relax her body from the shock she had expected.

"Let's see, the letter says that we overpaid our taxes because of an error in computation. Well, praise the Lord! At least my math errors worked in our favor this time. With this we'll be able to pay off some debts and still have some of the money in your account left. Let's go out and celebrate tonight."

"No way," Naomi responded. "That's the kind of thinking that got us into this fix in the first place."

"Just kidding," Ben said with a big grin. "I would much rather stay home and celebrate with my family."

Two weeks later, Ben and Naomi were back in Bryan Stanford's office. "Well, I'm really glad to see you two again," he began. "Obviously your presence here means you have decided to work together on your financial problems. I'll be honest with you. About half of the couples the pastor sends to me don't ever come back after the first meeting. They are looking for either a guaranteed miracle or some kind of quick fix. But if you didn't get into debt in three months, you won't get out of debt in three months. And as far as miracles go, I have seen God move in miraculous ways, but the more common approach is that He allows those who violate His principles to work their way out. Somehow the lessons seem to stick a lot better that way."

"We're not looking for a miracle or a quick fix," Ben said. "I know I created this mess by my own ignorance and childishness. I'm willing to do whatever is necessary to solve this once and for all."

"What about you, Naomi?" Mr. Stanford asked.

"I'm committed to the Lord, my husband, and whatever else it takes—in that order," Naomi said confidently. "I have already closed my account and put the surplus in our joint account."

"Good for you. I believe Ben is going to be worthy of your trust, and I know God will honor your faith. Now let's get down to business."

"First, we would like to ask a couple of questions," Ben said.

"Go ahead."

"As you may have guessed, we haven't been attending a church regularly for the past year or so. But we made a commitment to join Pastor Rhimer's church last week. Naomi feels very strongly that we should begin to tithe again. I want to too, but I can't figure out where the money would come from, even with the two new debts paid. Can we tithe even if it means we can't meet the obligations of the Chapter 13?"

"I commend your commitment to join a good church and to tithe the Lord's portion, but when you signed the court decree, you pledged yourself to the plan you submitted. You can't legally break your commitment and remain under the plan.

"As I see it you have two choices. You can elect to come out from under the Chapter 13 plan and take your chances with the creditors. Or you can reduce your own living expenses enough so you can tithe and still meet your obligations."

"How can we do that?" Ben asked. "There is no extra money available, except the small amount Naomi was saving, but even that should go to buy some clothes for Timmy and her."

"I think we're jumping ahead a little here. Let me tell you what I think, and maybe some questions will be answered." The coach jotted some numbers down on a piece of paper and showed it to Ben and Naomi. "First, your combined incomes are approximately this much a month. Right?"

"Yes," Ben replied. "That's pretty close."

"And your net take-home pay is about this much?" he continued, writing on the paper.

"I don't really know," Ben replied.

"Yes it is," Naomi chimed in.

"Okay," Bryan said. "Your overall housing expense, including utilities, comes to this amount per month." He leaned forward so the couple could watch as he worked some figures on paper. "That means it takes 56 percent of your net spendable income—income after tithe and taxes—just to maintain your home. The most you should spend on housing is 40 percent of your net spendable income. In your income category, we generally recommend 30 percent, but I'm allowing 40 percent because the cost of housing in this area is higher."

"I was convinced all along that our home cost us too much," Naomi said. "But I didn't know how to calculate what we could afford. The bank used 25 percent of our total incomes when we bought the house. But I was making more money then."

"Gross income doesn't mean a thing," Bryan answered. "It's what you have left over to spend that's important."

"Are you saying that we should sell our home and move to a cheaper one?" Ben asked.

"I'm not going to tell you to do anything, I'm just going to point out some logical alternatives. Then you'll have to make your own choices. I know that you get attached to your home—often a woman especially—and giving it up is a difficult decision."

"Not for me," Naomi said quickly. "I've always viewed that house as an anchor around our necks. It was Ben who really wanted it in the first place."

"That's probably true," Ben said. "But the guys at work said it was stupid to pay rent when I could buy a home and get all the tax breaks."

"Usually that's pretty good logic—but not when you wreck your budget to buy. It would be better to rent and stay within your income than to buy and end up in debt," Mr. Stanford said. "I believe you could potentially free up hundreds of dollars a month by renting for a while."

"That much!" Ben exclaimed. "That would be enough to pay our tithes and more. I guess I never realized the house was putting us into that much debt. I always thought of it as a good long-term investment."

"For most families it is. But only after they have settled into a lifestyle and found a home within their budget. Buying a home too quickly and one that is too expensive is the number one reason most young couples end up in financial trouble."

"But why doesn't someone tell people those things before they make the mistakes we made?" Naomi asked.

"In our society people make money off the excesses of others, unfortunately. However, there's a verse in Proverbs that presents the principle I'm talking about. I have it written on a card—Proverbs 24:27: 'Finish your outdoor work and get your fields ready; after that, build your house.' That means do the preparation first, before you plunge ahead before you're ready."

"I never heard that before," Ben said in amazement. "Let's put the house up for sale today."

"Hold it just a minute," Bryan said. "Don't do anything in haste. Pray about the decision together first, and if you think it's the right way to go, ask God to bring the right buyer for your home. Remember, there's no guarantee a house will sell quickly these days. You need to think about some other areas too. I'm going to give you a workbook that will help you plan each area of your budget. It's especially important that you allocate money for non-monthly expenses, such as clothes, car maintenance, and annual insurance. Those are normally areas that create crises when they are due."

"That's certainly true in our case," Naomi said.

"We want your budget to be totally realistic, or it will only work a short while. You're going to be tight on money until some of your past debts are paid. But with some discipline you will be debt-free in a few years.

"I have one additional recommendation for you. I believe Naomi is far better equipped to maintain the records and pay the bills. The short personality test I gave you last time shows that she is a detail person, but you, Ben, are a generalist."

"Yeah, I'd have to agree," Ben said, "but I always thought that it is the man's responsibility to handle the finances in his family."

"Ben, God gives each of us gifts and abilities to help us in our daily lives. It's clear that Naomi is better suited to be the bookkeeper in your family. The two of you together need to work out a financial plan, and then she will pay the bills and maintain the records. God doesn't make mistakes; He provided the necessary talents in Naomi that you lack, and vice versa. I suggest that you read Proverbs 31 together, because it describes a husband and wife working as a team. It's clear that each uses different and unique abilities to enhance the relationship.

"Our short-term goal will be to get your finances to the point that you're able to pay everyone what you owe them each month. That will mean Naomi will need to continue to work, at least for a while. But our long-term goal will be to free you financially so that Naomi can stay home to be a full-time mom if she wants to be. And you should set up a retirement plan."

"But we have tried that before. Every time I quit working we fell further and further behind," Naomi said.

"That's because you started out with expenses larger than your income. I believe you'll find when you readjust your budget that you'll be able to get by on one income. Later, if you want to return to the workplace, you should use your income only for one-time purchases."

"What do you mean?" asked Ben.

"Save it and buy a car, or save it for a down payment on a home, but don't commit yourselves to monthly expenses based on two incomes, especially at your age."

"That's one lesson we've learned the hard way," Ben replied, looking at Naomi.

"I want you to go home with the plan I have given you and make the necessary adjustments in your budget. Remember that each and every category of spending must have some money allocated to it. To ignore areas like entertainment and recreation is unrealistic and will cause your budget to fail within a short period of time. Ignoring needs like clothing, auto repairs, and dental bills will make your budget look good but will also make it totally unrealistic."

"What about giving?" Naomi asked. "I always tithed before I was married, but we've been unable to for most of our marriage."

"Tithing is an important principle for a Christian; it demonstrates a commitment to God in the most visible area of our lives: money. But God wants you to honor your word also. You have made an agreement with the court to pay your creditors according to the budget you submitted, so you must do so. One part of your long-term plan should be to reduce your monthly expenses so that later you can give God His portion too. But for now you'll have to stick to the plan you have. I believe God will honor the commitment in both of your hearts. He doesn't care about the money nearly as much as He cares about heart attitude. Tithing will be a part of the next stage of financial planning for you and Ben, once the expenses are reduced."

THEIR PLAN

I trust that by now you recognize the errors that Ben and Naomi made in their finances. Their problem could be called "too much, too soon." It is a common malady for many young couples in our society. It has been said (and unfortunately is all too true) that a young couple today tries to accumulate in three years what took their parents thirty years to accumulate. The one thing that people, both married and single, need to learn very quickly is that individuals must be self-disciplined. They cannot count on the lenders to force them to live within their means.

Unfortunately, some young couples have no idea how to calculate what they can or cannot afford to pay. So, they end up taking out mortgages that consume an excessive amount of their household income. Combine that with the use of second mortgages to help make the down payments and loans for refrigerators, lawn mowers, and curtains, and you can see why so many young couples have ended up in financial trouble.

But the purpose of this book is not only to show how people can get into debt, it is to help you understand how to get out of debt. To do that, we need to follow Ben and Naomi as they carry out the plan their financial coach worked out with them.

First, it's important to understand that by the time they went to see him they were deeply in debt and had elected to file for a Chapter 13 reorganization under the Federal Bankruptcy Code. The chart below is a summary of Ben and Naomi's financial condition when their coach Bryan Stanford first saw them. The figures on the left reflect what Ben and Naomi had budgeted. The figures on the right represent a better distribution of their money.

As you can see, Ben and Naomi had a financial problem that could be solved only by creating more income or by spending less. Since more income wasn't an option for them, they had to spend less.

In reality, less spending is the answer for the vast majority of debt problems. Most of us would be able to spend almost unlimited amounts of money, given the chance; so, more money coming in usually means more money going out.

Ben and Naomi Wister's "As Is" budget compared to a Recommended Spending Plan for a family with a gross monthly income of $5,500

THE WISTERS' "AS IS" BUDGET		RECOMMENDED SPENDING	
Taxes (taken out)	$1,595	Taxes	$1,595
Tithe	$0	Tithe	$550
Housing	$1,900	Housing	$1,345
Auto	$625	Auto	$300
Food	$400	Food	$400
Clothing	$0	Clothing	$75
Medical	$0	Medical	$100
Insurance	$100	Insurance	$100
Entertainment/Recreation	$0	Entertainment/Recreation	$85
Debt	$300	Debt	$0
Miscellaneous	$150	Miscellaneous	$150
Savings	$0	Savings	$200
School/Childcare	$600	School/Childcare	$600
Total	$5,670	Total	$5,500

A glance at the Wisters' "As Is" budget tells much of the story. Their budget could have handled the spending of up to 40 percent of their net pay for housing (about $1,350 per month including utilities), but they had committed themselves to payments that were 56 percent of their net income (income remaining after deducting taxes and tithes), or $1,900 per month. They had difficulty making it on such a budget, even from the beginning.

Note also that they were overcommitted in the Auto and Debt categories. Those debts were the obvious result of the amount of money eaten up each month by the high house payment. When necessities came up—such as clothes, insurance, or car repairs — Ben used credit to make up the difference. The overcommitment he made regarding the cars reflected a weakness in Ben toward cars. His weakness in this area is not unusual — in fact it is quite common in most young men. During the dating years in high school and college, they place such great importance on their automobiles that they become personal status symbols. That's a poor attitude when Mom and Dad are paying the bills and the young person is still single, but it is a disaster when the young man gets married and continues to cling to the same values.

When you look at the budget for Clothing, Entertainment/Recreation, and Medical expenses, you will note that Ben and Naomi allocated nothing on a regular monthly basis for those items. That doesn't mean they found a miraculous way to keep their clothes from wearing out or their teeth from developing cavities. It means they didn't have money for those items, so they left them out of their budget. When these expenses came due — as they were bound to — Ben and Naomi had to rely on credit cards to make up the deficit. That is why so many couples say they use their credit cards only for necessities. Often that's true, except that other spending creates the need to use the cards for the necessities.

Bryan Stanford gave Ben and Naomi some suggestions to help them resolve both their immediate and their long-term problems.

1. Use the funds they already had on hand to pay the Visa bill and the outstanding balance on the car Ben had returned. Mr. Stanford made direct contact with the owner of the car lot and told him what had happened with Ben. In this case, the owner generously agreed to negotiate for a reduced amount in total payment of the bill.

2. Each month continue to meet the obligations established by the bankruptcy court. With Ben and Naomi's combined incomes, they were able to pay at least the minimum amounts due.

3. Make a budget showing what they could afford to pay for housing. This showed how totally out of line their housing expenses were with

their income. They decided to sell the house, and because of a decline in housing values, they received just enough to cover what they owed. They paid off their mortgage and began renting until they could get back on their feet.

4. Assign Naomi the task of managing the books in their home. She would pay the bills each month, and she and Ben would review the budget together at least once a month.

5. Once the bankruptcy payments were completed, make a budget that they could live with.

After three years, when the last creditor was repaid, Ben and Naomi used her income for several months to repay the tithes they had not been able to pay before. Their coach, Bryan, told them that as far as he could tell, Scripture did not require or suggest a repayment of past tithes and offerings. After praying about what he said, they still committed themselves to repaying their tithes as a testimony that God truly was first in their marriage.

C H A P T E R

UNDERSTANDING
BUD *and* SANDI

Bud Hawkins was a responsible person who tried to better himself and provide his family with a comfortable lifestyle. He came from a relatively poor background—the family never seemed to have enough money, and what there was had to stretch to accommodate a big family—where he was pretty much left to fend for himself. When he finished high school he found a job, and saved as much money as he could. After two years he started at a junior college in his hometown, continuing to work.

While he was in college, he had worked nearly full-time in the evenings and on weekends. He wasn't a straight-A student, but he made fairly good grades. He was sure he could have done even better if he had had more time to study.

Bud and Sandi met when he was at the state university, completing his last two years of college. They were married during his last year in school. They had a nice off-campus condominium her parents had bought her when she went to college.

Though Sandi's father was a very successful trial attorney, her parents didn't consciously indulge her. They simply included her in their upscale lifestyle that meant a new wardrobe each year, a new car every other year, and winter vacations in Colorado.

She knew other people didn't have as much as her parents, because she had several close friends who came from middle-income families. But she also experienced strife in her own family because her mother and father argued frequently. Usually their arguments revolved around her father's commitment to his work and the fact that he was rarely around. Many times Sandi, her mother, and one of Sandi's friends spent those holiday trips to Aspen or Vail without Sandi's father. He rarely accompanied them. By the time Sandi was a senior in high school, her parents were separated. The separation later became semipermanent, although there was never a divorce. Her mother did not cope well.

In college, Sandi's life was radically changed through a campus ministry. She was invited to a meeting and agreed to go because she already considered herself a Christian. At that meeting she came face-to-face with the reality that she was a churchgoer, but not a Christian, and she accepted Christ.

At a later meeting she met Bud, fell in love with him, and married him within the year. As is so often the case, although Sandi was not the least bit embarrassed by her new husband's humble background, he was. Visiting her home was agony for Bud; it made him feel inadequate. Nothing she could say would convince him that all was not bliss in that beautiful home. His goal was set: eventually he would have the same kind of home.

I share this background to show that when someone gets into debt from seeking a "comfortable" lifestyle, it is often the result of decisions clouded by good intentions and rationalizations. I believe that one of the worst things that can happen to people is achieving their financial goals. Then they are able to surround themselves with enough "things" and consider themselves to have achieved a measure of happiness.

After college, Bud took a job with a major stock brokerage firm. He was a fast learner and had a pleasant personality, and he did quite well. But within a few years Sandi feared she was seeing the same attitudes developing in Bud that she had seen in her father. Bud was consumed by business and had a drive to succeed that pushed everything and everyone else into the background.

Sandi began to complain to Bud about his lack of care for his family and his noninvolvement in their lives.

The more Sandi protested, the less Bud knew how to handle it, so he began to substitute time at the office for time with her. As his income grew, so did opportunities to take part in some of the investments his company brokered. He began to risk larger amounts of borrowed money, secured only by his signature.

Within a few years, Bud's net worth had grown to a handsome six-figure number, and with it grew his ability to borrow even more. He bought a million-dollar home in a wealthy neighborhood — despite Sandi's objections.

Bud even made several attempts to spend more time at home, but too often another deal would develop, and he would spend weeks of sixteen-hour days putting it together. When she saw the volumes of forms that had to be filed with their tax statements each year, Sandi asked Bud to sit down and discuss their finances. Bud said he would, but he never took the time to do so. He knew that Sandi wouldn't agree with many of the things he was doing, so it was just easier to avoid telling her.

As time passed, Sandi felt more and more excluded from what had become the focus of Bud's activities. All she knew about their finances was how much Bud gave her to run the household. He was extremely generous, and Sandi usually got whatever she asked for.

Then suddenly the economy, which had been inflating the real estate ventures Bud was handling, cooled off. Interest rates for speculative real-estate deals rose precipitously. The real estate market that had grown as a result of borrowed money suddenly stopped cold.

Almost overnight, Bud found himself with virtually no income. Land sales had all but stopped, and the value of his holdings fell sharply. Banks that once welcomed Bud's business were suddenly inflexible. They were unwilling to restructure short-term loans secured by his land investments. They wanted their money back and they wanted it back now. The bankers already knew what Bud was about to find out: "The rich rule over the poor, and the borrower is servant to the lender" (Proverbs 22:7).

One bank, however, did offer Bud a deal. They would restructure his loans if he would sign over his house as substitute collateral. To do this, he needed Sandi's agreement, since the house was in both their names. Bud approached Sandi that evening after their kids had gone to bed. "Sandi, I've got a problem and I need your help," Bud said timidly.

Her mind conjured up the worst circumstances imaginable. "What kind of a problem, Bud?"

"Without a second mortgage on the house, the banks won't restructure some of the loans I have on the land investments. They say the land isn't worth enough anymore. So they want me to put up the house as collateral. Now, don't worry. That doesn't mean we have to move. It's just a banking thing. Just a piece of paper."

Sandi breathed a sigh of relief, but outwardly the tough shell she had assumed as a defense stayed intact as she answered in a biting tone, "And just how much do you owe on your great investments, Bud?"

Bud winced at her tone and at the emphasis she had placed on the words *your* and *Bud*. "I don't know exactly," he lied.

"Well, give me an approximate figure. Or do you think I'm too dumb to be trusted with information like that?" Sandi said with tears coming to her eyes in spite of herself.

"You know I don't think you're dumb," Bud said with his head down.

"Well, you must. You have never once told me what you're doing. I learn more at the Christmas party when your so-called partners are there than I do living in the same house with you."

Bud didn't know where to go with the conversation. They had been at this point before. He had wanted to tell Sandi what he was doing and why, but when she took such an offensive position, he just backed off and buried himself in his work. But he couldn't do that now. If he didn't sign over the house as collateral, the bank could call his loans immediately. He would lose everything. Worse than that, he would probably still owe hundreds of thousands of dollars after the properties were sold in this down market. He knew if he could hold on and ride out the bad times, the land values would recover. But right now, the house was the only thing of value he had to pledge. "Listen, Sandi, I know you've been hurt by my actions in the past, but this is a real crisis. If I can't give the banks some additional collateral, they will call the notes on the properties and sell them at cut-rate prices," Bud said as honestly as he could.

"You still didn't answer my question, Bud. How much do you owe?"

As he started to speak, Bud flinched at what he knew would be a verbal assault from Sandi. "I owe nearly $800,000," he said.

And to his utter amazement, he heard Sandi reply, "Well good, then we'll be totally broke when this thing is over, I suspect. I'll be glad to see it all gone."

"Why?" Bud asked, puzzled.

"Because I've been praying for a long time that something would happen to bring all this to a head. We aren't married; we're just two people living in the same house, sharing the same bed.

"You really don't understand, do you?" she continued, as Bud looked away. "I don't care about the money, the house, or anything money can buy. I would be perfectly satisfied in a three-bedroom house in a simple subdivision with a husband who came home at five o'clock and spent time with his family. Bud, what am I going to do after our kids leave and I'm left here by myself? My mother started drinking because she couldn't stand her life. I don't know what I'd do."

Because of the emotional state he was in, Bud didn't hear what Sandi was really trying to say. All he heard was his wife saying she wished she had married someone else. In an attitude of resignation he asked, "Will you sign the power of attorney on the house, Sandi?"

"You didn't hear a word I said, did you?" she declared, amazed. Was that all he'd gotten out of what she'd said? "Yes, I'll sign so you can get your loans renewed. I don't want to hurt you; I just want us to be one, and we're not. But I can tell you this: When the bottom falls out of your business, your so-called friends are going to leave you high and dry. Then what are you going to do, turn and run too?"

"I have never run from anything in my life," Bud responded. "I believe the investments I have made are sound, and I'll stand by the people who have invested with me, no matter what."

"You may get a chance to find out what 'no matter what' is," Sandi said. "Some clients sue their financial advisers during a bad time in the real estate market. Yours will too."

"The people who invest with me know that I always try to do what's best for them," Bud said defensively. "I can't help what happens to interest rates. They know that."

"Get into the real world, Bud," she said. "Those people won't care if you spend twenty hours a day working for them. What most of them care about is that you sold them an investment that lost money."

Bud pledged their home as collateral against the bank loans and was able to hold off the foreclosures for the time being. But several months passed, and the economic situation didn't get any better. In fact, it got worse. Many of the biggest banks had hundreds of nonperforming loans and began to experience financial problems themselves. Loan managers were fired or moved, and new management was brought in to deal with the crisis. All real estate loans that had not been paid on in more than three months were immediately called as due and payable — Bud's included.

It didn't matter what arrangements had been made in the past. The rule was, pay in full, or surrender the properties. In an effort to salvage some of the more valuable properties, Bud approached some of his wealthiest clients, who stood to lose the most if the ventures failed. He asked them to put up the necessary capital to collateralize the notes on the land they were already invested in. In exchange, he would subordinate his position (take a lesser profit after they got their money when the land was sold). He also guaranteed their additional collateral with a third mortgage on his home without telling Sandi.

Unfortunately, the interest rates remained high, and the real estate market dropped even further as desperate bankers dumped large inventories of unsold land on the already depressed market. Land prices dropped more than 70 percent from the pre-recession high. The investors Bud had convinced to put up additional collateral were faced with either risking more of their assets or losing what they had already pledged. They opted to lose what they had pledged and sue Bud and his partners for negligence.

Faced with the collapsed real estate market and a pending lawsuit, Bud's three partners elected to file for bankruptcy protection. It was only then that Bud learned that all of their personal assets were held in their wives' names and that, other than the now-defunct properties, they had no assets to lose. The investors were left with no one to go after except Bud.

Bud knew he had done nothing illegal or unethical in his dealings with his investors, and he was certain he would be vindicated if the case came to trial. He had been advised not to settle with the disgruntled investors, and they continued their suit out of anger and vindictiveness over the losses they had suffered.

Ultimately, the case came to trial, and Bud waived his right to a trial by jury so the case would be heard and decided by a single judge. The attorney for the investors depicted Bud as a scheming manipulator who had talked his clients into risking money in ventures they could not possibly understand. The conclusion the judge reached: guilty as charged.

The decision broke Bud. Not only was he judged to be guilty of defrauding investors, but his license to sell securities was suspended for five years. He was penniless and without the means to earn a living.

The judge allowed the plaintiffs to attach anything of value Bud owned now or in the future. They elected to force Bud into bankruptcy by notifying all of his outstanding creditors that they intended to attach and sell any and all properties he owned, including his house. Bud's other creditors quickly filed suit, trying to get at least some part of Bud's assets.

"Bud, you told me this lawsuit would amount to nothing, and now we have this judgment against us," Sandi said angrily. "Do you call this nothing?"

"Look, I told you I'm sorry." Bud sighed. "I wanted to tell you, but I just didn't know how. They're demanding a forced sale of the house and everything else. We'll be wiped out. I wouldn't blame you if you decided to leave. The SEC is suspending my license for five years because I lost the lawsuit; I won't even have a way to earn a living."

"Bud, I don't care about this house or the investments. I told you that before. I just want to be a part of your life. I will stick by you because we promised God that our marriage is for better or worse. I love you, and we'll be able to see this thing through together," Sandi said earnestly. The tears welled up in her eyes. "I was afraid you were going down the same path I saw my own father go down before he left my mother, and it frightened me."

"I'm so sorry, Sandi," Bud said as he put his arms around her. "I didn't know that's what you were thinking. I thought I was doing all these deals for you and the kids. Now I realize that I was doing them to feed my own ego and insecurity. I feared going back to always struggling, so much that I was willing to throw away the most important assets God ever gave me."

"Bud, we've drifted so far from God's path. I want to rededicate our lives to serving Him — like we promised to do in college."

"I agree," he said, as he felt a burden lift from his shoulders. "You know, it's funny, we're totally broke and facing bankruptcy, but I finally feel free. Maybe you have to hit bottom before you can begin to look up."

"I know this sounds crazy, but maybe we can use this as an opportunity to witness for the Lord. Why don't you go to each of the creditors and ask them not to force you into bankruptcy. Tell them that we intend to pay back every dime of the money, if they'll work with us."

"How can we do that?" Bud asked, looking at his wife with an air of appreciation. "We're dead broke, and I lost my license."

"Then it's really up to the Lord to do it, isn't it?" Sandi asked.

"Well, you're right, it does sound crazy. But it's also kind of exciting. If any of the creditors are crazy enough to go along with us, it could really be a testimony to God's greatness. I'll just tell them the truth. If they join in the bankruptcy, they probably won't get anything. After all, the first and second mortgage will wipe out any money from the house, and the cars are leased. I'll start calling first thing tomorrow."

Bud went to each of the creditors, most of whom were banks holding deficiency agreements on the property loans, and asked them not to force him into bankruptcy. When he was asked how he would ever repay the money he owed, he responded, "I don't know, but if the Lord chooses to bless us, I'll repay every dime—if you don't join in the bankruptcy action. In the meantime I'll get a job and pay you what I can each month."

Bud's biggest creditor was the largest bank in town. Based on the current value of the land they had foreclosed, the bank estimated Bud owed them over $400,000. He met with the bank president (a former client) and asked him not to join in the bankruptcy action.

"But, Bud, I have a responsibility to our stockholders," was the banker's reply. "If you're hiding any assets and we don't join the lawsuit, I could be sued for negligence."

"I give you my word that what you see on the paper before you is everything I own in the world, and it isn't much," Bud said.

"But why don't you want me to join in the lawsuit, Bud? If this is all you own and our agreement is thrown into the bankruptcy too, you won't have to repay us either."

"Because my wife has convinced me that God can show Himself strong through this," Bud replied with confidence. "My part is to ask my creditors to trust me as I trust the Lord."

Bud then shared Psalm 50:14–15, a passage he and Sandi believed God had given to them the night they pledged to repay everyone who did not join the bankruptcy action: "Sacrifice thank offerings to God, fulfill your vows to the Most High, and call upon me in the day of trouble; I will deliver you, and you will honor me."

"Well, Bud, that's about the strangest proposal I have ever heard in my years as a banker, but I'm a Christian too, so . . ." Bud waited as the banker thought. "Tell you what—I'll take this to my board of directors at our meeting this Thursday. I'll recommend we go along with you on this, but the final decision is up to the board."

"I understand, and I sincerely appreciate your confidence in me," Bud said as he started to leave.

"Bud, I believe you're an honest man, and you always did a good job for me. You made errors in judgment on some of the land deals we funded, but who hasn't? You borrowed too much on speculation, but frankly we lent too much on the same projects."

"Thank you. That really does encourage me. I trust we'll both see some miracles."

Later that week Bud heard from the banker that the board had agreed to maintain their notes and not join the bankruptcy.

The bankruptcy proceeded rapidly, with all but three creditors joining in the proceeding. Bud and Sandi did not contest the bankruptcy action and surrendered all of their personal assets voluntarily, including personal jewelry, even their wedding rings. The bankruptcy judge instructed them that they had the right to maintain ownership of certain personal assets, such as the wedding rings, but they refused, saying they wanted the creditors to receive as much as possible.

Ultimately, the disgruntled investors who had brought the action received almost nothing for their trouble once the legal bills were paid.

In the meantime, Sandi was pleased to find a part-time job in a nearby hospital's insurance office. Bud searched for a job that would allow him to provide for his family. He decided eventually that selling was the only thing he knew how to do, and he took a job on a commission basis in product sales with a national company. Within three months he had met the minimum quota set by the company but was earning an average annual income of far less than he had earned before. He and Sandi worked out a budget that would allow them to live under this amount, with the rest going to pay the creditors they still owed from the land deals as well as the large bank.

Bud and Sandi settled into a greatly modified lifestyle and committed themselves to getting to know each other better and discovering what the Lord had in store for them.

❍ ❍ ❍

Bud had violated two fundamental biblical principles that ultimately resulted in his financial disaster: Falling for a get-rich-quick scheme and ignoring his top adviser.

GET RICH QUICK

Symptoms of a get-rich-quick mentality are evident in many investment ideas. There are three distinguishing characteristics.

Risking Borrowed Money

If investments in get-rich-quick schemes were limited to available cash only, most people would be wary of losing it. But somehow it's easier to risk *borrowed* money, because it seems almost free — at least until you have to pay it back. The same principle applies to buying consumer goods on credit. Credit card companies understand the mentality of leveraged purchases (purchases bought with borrowed money). People who use their credit cards for clothing, food, and vacations are prime candidates for overbuying. Credit card issuers can prove to a merchant, statistically, that those people will buy more and pay a higher price than those who buy only with cash.

There is no argument that through the use of leveraged (borrowed) money you can get rich a lot faster. But there also is no argument that the majority of those who do that end up losing it all in the long run. The mentality that prompted them to take the initial risk will prompt them to take ever bigger risks, and eventually they could get wiped out in a bad economy. The Bible says, "The plans of the diligent lead to profit as surely as haste leads to poverty" (Proverbs 21:5).

You don't have to look any further than the housing industry in America to verify that principle. Thousands of homeowners were wiped out when the housing bubble popped between 2007 and 2009. They had overborrowed to buy houses in an inflated market. When the bottom fell out, they ended up owing more than their houses were worth. Many lost everything.

How did this happen? Briefly, in the early 2000s, the housing market was flourishing. Individuals would get their mortgage loan from a broker, who would sell the mortgage to a bank. The bank would then sell the mortgage to a Wall Street investment firm. A firm would then have thousands of payments from mortgages coming in monthly, which they could use for investment.

As demands for mortgage-backed securities grew, lenders began to lower qualifications for individuals obtaining mortgages. No longer must a buyer have a down payment, so more and more people were purchasing houses as investments, intending to turn them around for a profit. This practice created more demand for housing, thus pushing up prices. If people were unable to make their mortgage payments, they could simply take out another loan against the value of their home, since it was now worth more. Home equity loans and lines of credit were increasingly common.

Unfortunately, though the price of houses was going up, household incomes were not. Property values no longer increased, and the lenders found that many people were defaulting on their mortgages. Thus, the number of houses on the market increased, pushing prices down. Many individuals and families found that their homes were foreclosed on, or that they owned a house that was worth less than they owed on it.[1]

Getting Involved with Plans When You Don't Know the Full Story

The second element of the get-rich-quick mentality—taking financial risks in fields you know little or nothing about—is dangerous if there is any possibility of losing sizable amounts of money in the investment.

Financier Bernard Madoff was able to fool thousands of wealthy investors into believing he had developed an investing method that could make lots of money in both good times and bad. It was largely a hoax. His clients lost millions.

Some people are particularly vulnerable to being tricked by foolish schemes because they tend to trust anyone who claims to be a Christian, especially if he or she claims to have a special "revelation" from God. Beware of anyone who is selling something and says, "I was praying about this idea, and God told me to call you."

One classic scam has been going around the Internet for many years. You receive an e-mail from a foreign country, sent by someone who claims to be a former government official or the widow of a fabulously wealthy businessman. The government official has been forced from office, or the oppressed widow is being illegally separated from her money—you get the idea. But you can do a good deed, they say, and help these unfortunates move their untold millions out of their country into a safe account (yours), and in return, they'll thank you by rewarding you with a high percentage of their fortune.

You'll need to send a "facilitation fee," however. And something will go wrong to hold up the transaction. So you'll have to send in more money, again and again, until you've sent thousands. You'll receive nothing in return.

Another take on this scam, called "4-1-9," "advance fee fraud," and other names, targets churches or other religious organizations. In this variation of the scheme, the e-mailer will desire to leave his fortune to that group. Perhaps he wants his fortune to further the good work they do, or, tugging on heartstrings, the writer says he's led a sinful life, has become a Christian, and wants to make up for his evil deeds. But the well-meaning beneficiary of this windfall must still send money, which is never enough, and probably supply banking information. More requests for facilitation fees will be sent until the bank account is gone, and the wealthy donor disappears.

Incredibly, intelligent people are still falling for this scam. Jesus was right to warn, "I am sending you out as sheep in the midst of wolves, so be wise as serpents and innocent as doves" (Matthew 10:16 ESV).

Examples of Ponzi or pyramid schemes abound. Basically, these plans involve the promise of a high return on an investment over a short period of time, with more and more investors or givers being recruited to support those already in the program. "Cash gifting," "gifting program," "matching gift" are some of the terms used in schemes that are especially attractive to Christians or others who believe their money is going to good causes. We need to be wise in evaluating any financial plan, especially one that may take advantage of our tendency to be trusting of anything that labels itself "Christian" or that promises incredibly great returns.

Making Hasty Decisions

Bud Hawkins set aside something he understood and knew how to do well (selling securities), and moved into an area where he was less skilled (land investments). He started putting together quick deals without careful evaluation. It wasn't that Bud was trying to deceive anyone. He was just trying to make a lot of money and make it fast. Indeed, the judge ruled that there came to be an inherent conflict between Bud's interests (putting together a "deal") and the interests of his clients.

Bear in mind what God's Word says about a get-rich-quick attitude. "A faithful man will be richly blessed, but one eager to get rich will not go unpunished" (Proverbs 28:20).

I said that Bud had violated two basic biblical principles in his finances. The first was having a get-rich-quick attitude. The second was ignoring the primary adviser the Lord had provided, his wife, Sandi.

IGNORING YOUR TOP ADVISER

I don't think I can stress this principle too strongly. It is dangerous for a husband or wife to ignore the principal adviser the Lord has given: a spouse. In His infinite wisdom, God created humankind as male and female. He didn't have to—after all, He did create some asexual creatures with no need of a mate or a friend. But I suspect they lead rather dull lives.

When you live with someone in a relationship as close as husband and wife, there are bound to be problems. Since opposites tend to attract, you may not agree about everything. In fact, you may never totally agree about anything. But that's okay, as long as you know how to work it out together and reach a reasonable compromise.

Bud's background made him a candidate for excesses in the area of finances. Often it is not the person from a wealthy background who is obsessed by success but rather the one from a modest or poor background. We all have the tendency to overcompensate for what we lacked as children.

I came out of a relatively poor background in a wealthy community, and I tend to store rather than spend. Fortunately, God blessed me with a wife who prefers to sit on real furniture, or I would probably be sitting on orange crates. She helps to balance my extremes, and I balance hers.

These distinctive personality types should not be ignored when a couple works out the decision-making function in their marriage. We Christians have tended to stereotype the roles of husband and wife, but when we do that, we ignore the totality of God's Word on the subject and fail to recognize psychological realities.

The Scriptures do not draw an exact parallel between home relationships and the church. Instead, when the totality of God's Word is considered, and not just isolated passages, it is evident that mutual decision-making is a more accurate description of the Bible's counsel on the matter. Genesis 2:18 indicates that the woman should be a suitable helper for her husband. In 1 Peter 3:7 the husband is warned to treat his wife with consideration and respect, "so that nothing will hinder" his prayers. When a husband avoids or ignores his wife's counsel on any matter, including finances, he should expect his prayers to be hindered. The same can be said for a wife who does not give her husband the respect that God has assigned him as the head of his family.

Thus the stereotype does not work when it tends to diminish the balance God builds into a marriage. If the husband is the dominant personality and the primary decision maker, there is still the danger that he will tend to exclude his wife from financial decisions, investments, and major purchases.

But the stereotype completely breaks down when the husband is not naturally a dominant person. Sometimes he is, but in a high percentage of the families I have counseled, the wife is the dominant personality and the decision maker. Does that mean that God made an error in giving her a dominant personality and her husband a subdued personality? No, but it does mean that the wife in such a marriage must learn to listen to the counsel of her husband, just as dominant husbands must listen to their less dominant wives. If the wife hasn't learned to do this, she will be seen as pushy and domineering, rather than respectful. God created husband and wife to function as a single working unit, each with different but essential abilities. Certainly those abilities will overlap in many areas, and often that will lead to differences of opinions. But just as certainly, without the balance that each can bring to the marriage, great errors in judgment will be made.

It has been my observation that a dominant woman operating without the balancing influence of her husband will accumulate debt through credit cards and store accounts, because she buys too many clothes or household items. A dominant husband operating without the balancing influence of his wife will accumulate debt through the purchase of a boat, motorcycle, or high-end electronics. Men don't buy very often, but when they do, they buy big.

Facing a Chapter 7 Bankruptcy with Prudence and Honor

Although the consequences of a Chapter 7 bankruptcy are very severe, a bankruptcy may indeed occur when a get-rich-quick scheme fails.

Bud and Sandi experienced the total dissolution of their assets through a creditor-initiated bankruptcy action. In Bud's case, he filed bankruptcy rather than allow the few demanding creditors to sell off his remaining assets to their benefit and to the detriment of all the others.

A bankruptcy action usually will provide only a fraction of the total debt owed to creditors, but creditors are required to accept the liquidation proceeds as total settlement of their debt. Again, in Bud's case, he and Sandi committed themselves to repaying everyone who agreed not to join the bankruptcy action. They felt that those creditors who elected to take the bankruptcy proceeds did so voluntarily and thus settled the debt.

To be as fair as possible to the creditors who joined the bankruptcy, Bud and Sandi retained no salable assets.

Unlike many others who file bankruptcy for their convenience, Bud placed all assets held in Sandi's name into the asset pool as well. They withheld nothing from the creditors.

Bankruptcy is never an action to be taken lightly. The financial consequences and the damage to a reputation are long-lasting for anyone, but especially for a Christian. A creditor has a right to expect to recover the money loaned in good faith, and the Bible is clear in its admonition to honor one's vows (promises). I believe that Bud and Sandi fulfilled this scriptural principle by going to each of the creditors and explaining why they decided to file for bankruptcy. They believed that the disgruntled investors would force them to sell off all their assets and that the unsecured creditors had a right to a share, if they so elected.

However, when Bud and Sandi approached the creditors, they also explained their total financial situation and indicated that the sale of all their assets would yield only a small fraction of the total debt. They then asked each creditor not to join the bankruptcy action on the promise (in writing) that they would repay all debts in total at a future date.

This action was taken against the counsel of their attorney, who recommended that they place all debts in the bankruptcy and clear them. He said they could choose to repay the deficiencies later, if and when they had the funds. Bud and Sandi decided not to take his advice, because they thought it should be the choice of the creditor to take what was available immediately or trust them to repay later.

Because of the loan defaults as a result of the bankruptcy, Bud also owed nearly $100,000 in taxes to the IRS. Under a rule called Forgiveness of Debt, most of the unrecovered loan balances were declared income and, as such, were subject to taxes, interest, and penalties.

Needless to say, Bud and Sandi felt like the weight of the world had been dropped on them. But they remembered Romans 13:1, 6–7: "Everyone must submit himself to the governing authorities, for there is no authority except that which God has established. The authorities that exist have been established by God. . . . This is also why you pay taxes, for the authorities are God's servants, who give their full time to governing. Give everyone what you owe him: If you owe taxes, pay taxes; if revenue, then revenue; if respect, then respect; if honor, then honor."

From that evening on, they made a commitment to pray that the IRS agent who was working on their case would come to know Jesus as his Savior. And they prayed that God would ultimately provide the funds to retire all their debts.

Three years passed as Bud and Sandi continued to pay on obligations that accumulated thousands of dollars in interest each year. Fortunately, Bud did product sales, and his annual income increased nicely. They were able to accelerate payments to the bank and to the IRS, and they also increased the amount they gave to the Lord. One day Bud was in his office when he got a call from the president of the bank.

"Bud, could we have lunch tomorrow? I'd like to talk to you about your outstanding loans."

"Sure," Bud replied somewhat apprehensively. He imagined all kinds of things. Perhaps the bank had decided to sue him for collection. *But that doesn't make any sense. I don't have any assets to sell. We're living in a rented*

house and driving an eight-year-old car. And, I've been making regular pay-
ments for years now.

That evening Bud and Sandi, together with their children, prayed for God's will in their lives, whatever that might be. Bud was able to go to sleep with the confidence that comes only from complete trust in God.

The next day at lunch Gary Cross, the bank president, said, "Bud, I want to thank you for living up to my confidence in you. I have to tell you that I had a dickens of a time convincing the other members of the board to go along with your plan. Some thought you were pulling a fast one on us. And others thought it would be better to get the whole thing over with and write off the bad debts. But your commitment and dependability to make a pay-ment each month has been the subject of praise at several board meetings over the last two years."

"Thank you, Gary. But I don't think I deserve any praise for doing what is my responsibility anyway," Bud replied honestly.

"Perhaps not, but I'll tell you this: Not one other major debtor to the bank has repaid any of the bad syndicated loans. Most of them went bankrupt and put all their assets in someone else's name. Doing what is right is not the norm today. We recently had a contract on the land you surrendered on your loans. Two days ago we sold the land, thus clearing your notes totally."

"What?" Bud said breathlessly. "You mean that—oh man! Hey, I under-stand you didn't have to do that. I'm just speechless."

"But that's not all," the banker continued. "Our board wants you to come to work for us and manage our foreclosed properties. And furthermore, I'm pretty sure we can pay you a good bit more than what you're earning now."

When he got to the car, Bud called Sandi. "Honey, this is truly an answer from the Lord. Thank you for teaching me about trusting Him."

"We've *both* learned to trust Him," she said. "Thank You, Jesus."

To conclude this particular couple's story, Bud did such a good job at the bank that eventually he was promoted to asset manager of the holding com-pany's properties. It took quite awhile, but the IRS debt was finally paid off, and Bud and Sandi could look back on the whole series of events as something for which they were now grateful. They had grown closer together, learned to depend on God's grace, and their children saw firsthand how people who had committed themselves to the Lord could persevere through difficult times, trusting that God would provide.

CHAPTER 8

JACKSON and LINN:
IF YOU FAIL *to* PLAN...

The financial troubles of the third couple discussed in this book, Jackson and Linn Reede, look at first as if they were the result of circumstances the couple could not control. Surely no one could have foreseen the medical problems their son would have or that the bills for his care would be so high. An argument could be made that the expenses they had for him would have wrecked anyone's budget.

But the fact is that Jackson and Linn's financial troubles were the result of poor planning. Although they were intelligent and committed people, they had never been taught the basics of finances. They had never measured Jackson's income against normal monthly expenses, and they had made no provision for any emergency spending they might someday have to make. The only way the couple made it financially was to use Linn's income to balance the budget.

This basic fact was not obvious to Jackson and Linn, and as a consequence, the steps they took as they began to slip into debt were ones that made a bad situation worse.

Shortly after the baby was born, Jackson and Linn's church took up a collection to help them with the additional hospital expenses. However, the extent of the medical bills was far beyond the means of their small church, and soon the bills were accumulating again. Jackson remembered Dr. Yuan's advice to consider filing for bankruptcy. Two other Christians also counseled Jackson to file for bankruptcy—to relieve some of the financial pressure.

In the meantime, the couple found that they were unable to meet their mortgage payments and the payments on a small debt on some furniture they had purchased. But since they had no real budget, they naturally assumed their financial problems were the result of the baby's medical expenses.

They soon began to develop an "I don't care" mentality about their finances. They assumed the situation was hopeless. Even though they continued to pray about their needs, they adopted the attitude of many Christians: praying but doubting if God would really answer.

They began to use their credit cards to fill the gaps in their budget. Jackson bought his gas on credit and ate out on credit; Linn bought baby supplies and groceries on credit. Without realizing it, they had adopted an attitude of despair and a philosophy that bankruptcy was inevitable. With no visible means to repay, they were running up bills and living beyond their means. Although the couple never would have robbed a bank, they were in effect doing the same thing: stealing from their creditors.

Seven months after Jordan was born, the couple was beginning to reap the seeds they had sown. Creditors were calling daily because nearly all their bills were delinquent. Two credit card companies had filed judgments against them, which they had ignored because they felt there was nothing that could be done anyway. When Jackson's pay was garnished, he was called into the office of the school administrator, Nick Swartz. "Jackson, I just received a notice of attachment from the court," Nick said solemnly. "I have to comply with the request and withhold 20 percent of your net pay. Are you having financial problems?"

"Yes, I'm afraid so," Jackson responded a little defiantly. "It's the medical bills for the baby."

"We know the bills must be a problem for you and Linn, and we're working on something that might help. But the garnishment is the result of a judgment from a Visa bill. Is that related to the medical expenses?"

"No, not directly," Jackson said, looking down at the floor as he spoke. "We've had to use our credit cards for normal expenses during the last few months. But it all started because of the baby's problems."

Then Nick began to realize that Jackson had allowed the problems with the baby to distort his thinking. He said, "Jackson, I believe you have more financial problems than just the medical bills from the baby. I know we don't pay our teachers nearly what the public school systems do, and it's tough to make it on one salary, but you took the job knowing that, and now I suspect that even without the baby you would be in over your head. I want you to go to a financial coach and get a clear picture of where you are financially. There is a potentially embarrassing situation developing through this whole thing."

"How so?" Jackson asked. "Will I lose my job over the garnishment?"

"No," Nick responded. "We have neither the right nor the authority— nor the desire—to dismiss you for that reason. But with Linn not working, you would have a difficult time making ends meet even if all your finances were in perfect order. We do have some teachers supporting families on one salary, but they must be very careful and live on a strict budget. With this garnishment I know your budget won't make it. Do you have other debts besides the Visa?"

"Well, yes, we do," Jackson responded uncomfortably.

"More than three thousand dollars?"

"Well, yes, I guess so, but we've decided to file for bankruptcy anyway. The medical bills would make it impossible to live on my salary, no matter what," Jackson said with an air of finality.

"No one could argue with that," Nick said as he recognized Jackson's discouragement. "Jackson, as Christians, and especially as teachers, you and

I have a responsibility to demonstrate the attributes of Jesus to those around us. In the eyes of our generation, nothing is as visible as the way we handle our finances, and—"

"I agree," Jackson said, interrupting. "But God had to know our baby would need a lot of attention that would cost a great deal of money. Who's to say this is not His plan?"

"I would. And I'd say it even if our roles were reversed and it was my son with the health problems. I believe you have allowed your circumstances to overrule your first commitment—to the Lord."

"I'm sorry, but that's easy for you to say because it isn't your son, and you make more money than I do," Jackson said defiantly.

"That's very true. But I would hope that our faith is not built on what someone else does or doesn't have, or on what they would or wouldn't do in similar circumstances. You see, there will always be someone else who is better off than either of us and someone who has more money than both of us."

Again Jackson said, "That's easy enough to say when it's not your finances. But I don't see anyone paying our bills for us."

"Perhaps that is not entirely true, Jackson."

"What do you mean?"

"Several members of the school board and the faculty have put money in a trust fund for the medical bills you and Linn have incurred. We realize that you can't meet all your expenses. We have been paying something on the bills for the last two months now. Didn't you notice that the balances on your hospital and doctor bills have gone down?"

Jackson stopped cold. No, he hadn't noticed. He had been so caught up in his problems that he had taken an antagonistic stance in relation to most of the creditors and had ignored all of the notices they had been sending. Linn had commented several times that they should try to contact the major creditors and let them know that they were having some severe financial problems. Jackson had shrugged it off saying, "We can't pay them anyway. So what difference does it make?"

"Another thing," Nick continued. "One of the school board members learned that a grant may be available from a foundation that specializes in situations like yours. It's possible to acquire grant money to help with these medical bills and even for much of the care Jordan will need over the next several years. She wants to work with you and Linn to apply for it."

Jackson was speechless for the second time that day. "I don't know what to say."

"You don't need to say anything. We did what we did because we care. But now I fear that you have positioned yourself so that just paying the medical bills won't solve the problems anymore. You and Linn need to pray about what to do. But let me encourage you to seek good counsel and not listen to the counsel of those who look for the easy way out all the time."

Jackson was excited about going home and telling Linn the good news about the possibility of their medical bills being taken care of by the foundation. But as he drove home, a feeling of depression came over him. He realized that they would still owe on credit cards that they had used during the last few months. He began to accept the fact that they would be paying for their ignorance and lack of self-discipline, perhaps for years.

Linn wasn't home when Jackson arrived, so he decided to review some of the bills that had been sent during the last few weeks. Most of them were still in his desk drawer unopened. He opened the envelopes and began to sort the bills by date and amount. An hour passed as he sorted bills from gas cards, department store cards, and three major credit cards. When he totaled what he had found, he was shocked. Surely this must be some kind of mistake, he told himself. We can't possibly owe that much.

He totaled the stack of bills again, but the figure came out the same: $6,764.34. Almost $7,000! And he knew that he still hadn't found all the bills. He had been so sure they only owed a few hundred dollars that even $1,000 would have been a shock. But $7,000! It seemed impossible.

When Linn arrived home, she knew immediately that something was wrong. Jackson was still sitting at the desk, looking at the stack of bills in front of him. "What's the problem, Jackson?" she asked, afraid of hearing the answer.

"I received word from Nick Swartz today that members of the school board have set up a trust and have been paying down our medical bills. That's why we haven't been getting overdue notices from the doctors or the hospital," he said.

"That's great," Linn responded enthusiastically. "So what's the problem?"

"That's not all," Jackson continued in a somber mood. "He also said that there might be a foundation that will handle Jordan's medical expenses from this point on. That will help greatly, won't it? One of the members of the school board is going to help us apply."

Linn was overwhelmed by the news. "Why, that's wonderful! The Lord is meeting every need we have."

"Not quite," Jackson said. "I just totaled up the credit card debts. We owe nearly $7,000, and I know that's not all of it."

"That's impossible," Linn said faintly as she eased herself into a chair.

"Unfortunately, it's not. We also have a judgment against my wages, as of today. I feel so stupid, Linn. I've been living as if there were no tomorrow and no God. I guess I just assumed that we would have to resort to bankruptcy, so I didn't care how much debt we accumulated. God has been faithful to fulfill His end, but I failed to hold up my end."

"What is our alternative now?" Linn asked as she moved to put Jordan in his crib.

"Looks like we only have one. God stopped us from filing bankruptcy by removing any excuse we might have had. The debts we owe are a result of our own decisions, and I can't blame anyone but myself. I don't see how we can do anything but commit to paying all our debts."

"But how will we be able to do that on your salary alone?" Linn asked.

"I don't think we can. I'll just have to tell the school that I need to start looking for a new job. In the meantime I'll go to each of the creditors and ask for a reduced payment until I can generate more income. But we can't do much about the garnishment. That will come out of each paycheck until the bill is paid in full. It won't leave us a lot to live on, but we'll have to learn to do it. I want to cut up the credit cards, too. As long as we have them, we'll be tempted to use them. And I think we need to go back to driving one car. Maybe we can sell my car for enough money to clear the Visa and the garnishment."

"But my car has nearly 100,000 miles on it. Can we get by with a car that old?"

"We'll have to," Jackson said. "It's going to be tough for a while, but as I said, we'll just have to do it."

Jackson left the Christian school for a job as a teacher and coach at a public school. He and Linn went to see the financial coach Nick had suggested and worked out a plan with the creditors that allowed them some transition time. It was nearly two years before they began to see daylight in their finances, but in three years they were totally free of their consumer debt.

They developed a course on finances and budgeting and have taught it in their church. And before any couple can get married in their church, they must go through the classes on how to manage money God's way and then demonstrate that they can live on a budget. Jackson's desire is to one day be the head of a Christian school, where he can teach young people early on to handle their money and avoid making the mistakes he and Linn did.

CHAPTER

BACK *to* BETH *and* PENNY

Beth's situation also showed a lack of foresight, but the roots of her debt problem actually began in her childhood, after her father's death. Prior to that sad event, the family had been modest but comfortable, and the daughters didn't have to think about whether or not they could afford something. But then her mother had to work to support the family, something she had not been prepared to do.

Beth and her sister loved their mother and did not really mind helping her in the catering business. But seeds of discontent began to grow in Beth as she could no longer have the new clothes or other amenities she had been used to and that her friends still enjoyed. By the time she was an adult, she was tired of denying herself. Having seen her mother go from being a content homemaker to struggling to support a family, Beth prepared for a satisfying career in order to be able to support herself whether or not she later married. She succeeded professionally, but failed to plan for much beyond today—she used credit to purchase what she wanted and justified to herself that she needed it, rather than plan ahead and save.

Beth found a Christian credit counseling service on the Internet and made an appointment to see someone in her area. She was determined to make a change in her life and sought a Christian service so she would do it according to God's principles.

Beth's first impression when she met with the coach, Jeri McFarland, was relief. Ms. McFarland assured her that her situation was not unique and was not impossible. From the time she said, "Hi, I'm Jeri," to the end of the first appointment, Beth knew she had an advocate.

Before the meeting, Jeri had asked Beth to write out all her debts, the monthly payments, the total due on each credit card, her auto payment, the student loans she was still paying on, her rent, utilities, and everything else. It wasn't a pleasant exercise, but Beth was now confident that God was on her side and had led her to this credit counseling service.

Jeri went over Beth's list of debts and asked her questions about her income. Beth was paid a salary and did not receive monetary bonuses, so she had a consistent paycheck twice a month. Jeri determined that Beth's situation qualified her for the program: she had debt she could not pay in full with her monthly income, but did have a steady income and intended to pay creditors all of what she owed.

Jeri contacted the creditors on Beth's behalf and worked out a payment plan each accepted. She negotiated a new interest rate with the credit card companies so new charges weren't accumulating.

Beth set up affordable, automatic payments each month to the credit counseling service, along with a modest fee, which it in turn paid out to each creditor. Beth's rent and car payment were not included in the plan—but she was not behind in her rent, and she contacted the company who held her auto loan herself and worked out a way to put a reasonable amount extra on each payment until she was caught up.

The coach worked with her to develop a realistic budget, so she was able to live on her salary without accumulating more debt. At Beth's request, Jeri worked in a percentage she could give to her church, which would increase as she became closer to paying off her debts. By staying with the program, Beth will be debt-free within four years.

PENNY'S LIFE CHANGES

On Monday morning, Suzanne came directly to Penny's desk. "Got a minute?" she asked.

"Sure," Penny said, closing the door to her office. "What's up?"

"I wanted to ask you . . . I went to this church over the weekend and I wondered if you'd come with me next week."

Penny was surprised. She had a church. Suzanne knew that. She didn't go every Sunday, but she went at least once a month and on all special days. Her religion was part of her upbringing, part of her family's roots for many generations back, even back to the old days in Europe. She was a good person, but definitely didn't believe in talking about religion—if a person was religious, it was fine, but Penny felt it should be kept to oneself. But Suzanne had become one of her best friends, and she wanted to please her.

"Well, maybe," she answered. "Oh, wait, I can't. This next Sunday is a memorial for a parishioner who died one year ago, so I have to be here."

"Actually, this church has a service on Saturday evening. I'd really like you to come with me. How about it?"

"Church on Saturday? This isn't one of those wacko places, is it?"

"No, of course not," Suzanne assured her. "Do you think I'd go somewhere like that?"

So Penny agreed. She and Suzanne went to New Life Community the following Saturday. Penny had never experienced anything like it. People were friendly, and when someone read John 3:16 and invited the audience to put their own name in the verse—"For God so loved Penny"—she felt something new and unknown stirring within her.

Penny and Suzanne returned to the church for several weeks, and soon both young women had accepted Christ as their Savior and made a commitment to live for Him. Penny quietly told her parents and some of her cousins and other relatives about her decision, but continued to attend her family's church on most Sundays, while going to the services at New Life on Saturdays. She believed that her family would be more amenable to hear about her new faith if they saw that it didn't pull her away from them.

One day the message at New Life was about how not only her life belonged to Christ, but so did her money and possessions. The thought that the Lord could be interested in everyday matters like money was a new one for her. The pastor mentioned a class in managing finances according to God's principles, and Penny signed up. Since she had never followed up with the debt counselor she had found online, instead putting off the problem to think about it another time, she decided she might as well see what this church had to say on the subject.

The teachers of the class that met the next Saturday morning were a married couple, Tim and Natalie Brooker, who both worked for the same Christian financial planning company. They surprised Penny when they said that the Bible had more than 2,300 verses about money and possessions. She grew a little uncomfortable when the topic turned to debt, but took advantage of the offer of a confidential session with the couple for later that afternoon.

When Penny met with the Brookers, she explained how she had hoped the seminar with Thom Handleman would introduce her to a way to generate income that would work for her. But Tim asked, "Did you check out his reputation before you took the advice to purchase the silver?"

"Well, no," Penny admitted. "It sounded sensible. There wasn't anything wrong with doing that, was there?"

"Not the purchase itself, if you had had the money to spare, no." Penny shifted uncomfortably in her seat. "But there are other sources of advice on financial matters."

"Such as—?" Penny prompted him.

"Well, primarily after Scripture, I look at what Christian experts have to say," Natalie offered. "They not only seek and give godly counsel, but they have your best interests in mind."

"Another good source is the good old-fashioned newspaper," Tim added. "I've found that the more I read by mainstream, respected columnists, the greater discernment I develop to, well, to smell a rat . . . or at least to nose out advice that doesn't stand up to God's truth."

Penny was starting to feel overwhelmed, as though there was no way out of her situation. When she said so, Natalie and Tim both assured her that it was God's desire to bring her out of debt and that there were people who would help her do so.

The Brookers set Penny up with a Christian credit counseling service similar to the one Beth had gone to. With their help, she learned to set up and live within a budget, to save for purchases and emergencies, and to discipline herself from using her charge cards. They worked with her creditors to get the interest rates down to amounts that could actually be paid off, and, through hard work that she looked at as an adventure—and a few stumbles— Penny was debt-free within five years.

The best part of her new life, of course, wasn't just being free of the weight of debt—but was the freedom of walking with Christ, of finding the joy of giving, and of experiencing His provision.

C H A P T E R

BILL and ANDREA:
TIME *to* GROW UP

In this chapter I would like to look at another couple. Bill and Andrea were college students in their early twenties.

Though they both came out of middle-class homes with parents who were Christians, their expectations regarding finances were quite different. Neither had ever attended a course on personal finances. Although they had both worked at a variety of summer jobs for several years, neither had more than a general idea of how to handle a checking account.

They met at a rally held by a Christian group on their college campus and kept steady company thereafter. Both Andrea and Bill were attending college on a variety of loans and grants. By their senior year, their loans totaled nearly $20,000 each. Bill knew he would be expected to begin to repay his loans after graduation, because his dad had made that clear from the beginning. Since he felt he had little choice, he continued to accumulate school loans.

Andrea and her parents never discussed the repayment of the loans she was receiving. She assumed that her dad would pay them, like he had paid all her bills, but she never really gave it much thought. But then in the early part of her senior year Andrea's father died suddenly of a heart attack. Her mother was devastated by her loss and went into a prolonged state of depression. Andrea withdrew from school for the semester and then returned to finish her degree.

In the past, her father had always given her money for the incidentals she needed just before she left for school. Since her father was gone, Andrea approached her mother.

"Mom, I'll need some money for books and dorm fees," she said.

"Dad always handled the finances, honey. I don't know what you need. Why don't you take my credit card and get whatever is necessary. We'll work it out when you come home next time. Maybe Daddy's insurance will be settled by that time, and I'll know what we have."

Andrea's mom then handed her two credit cards: one for buying gas for her car and the other for general expenses. Although Andrea had never owned a card of her own, she had often used her mother's card to fill the family car or run errands for her mom. The cards had only her mother's initials and last name on them. Because Andrea had the same initials as her mother, the merchants never questioned her signature.

Back at school Andrea called home regularly to see how her mom was doing. She was still in a state of semi-shock, and Andrea called her almost every day. When the first month's phone bill came for Andrea's cell phone, she had gone over her minutes, so she paid the bill with the card her mother had given her.

Andrea needed some clothes for school and normally would have called and asked her dad for some money. Usually he sent her a check, and she would buy a pair of jeans and a blouse or two. Since she knew her mother was in no shape to answer questions, she decided to use the card this time. By the time she finished the shopping trip she had charged over several hundred dollars' worth of new clothes and had also charged a watch for Bill.

She and Bill had begun talking seriously about their plans after graduation. They knew they would get married, but beyond that had no definite plans for what they would do. Bill was earning a degree in music, and Andrea's degree in elementary education required her to intern for at least three months. Then her employment would depend on finding an opening in the school system near the college. Bill wanted to go on to graduate school and gain his master's degree so he could teach music at the college level.

During the next three months, Andrea fell into a routine of using her mother's credit card periodically to take Bill out to eat and buy him gifts. Then she had the brakes fixed on her car, again using the card. Without realizing it she began to develop a habit of small indulgences, using her mother's card to pay for them. None were particularly significant by themselves, but when totaled, they began to add up. The bills came to her mother's home, where she put them unopened on her desk; she just couldn't cope with the details of daily life yet.

Suddenly school was coming to an end and Andrea was faced with entering the workforce for the first time, which made her feel a bit panicky. She thought more and more about getting married. She feared that if they waited until summer, something might happen to keep them from getting married. That thought really shook her. She had lost her father; she couldn't stand the thought of possibly losing Bill too.

One evening she said to Bill, "Why don't we go ahead and get married? I know Mom is in no shape to take on a wedding, and I'm not sure she could emotionally handle seeing me get married anyway."

"But how will we make it financially?" Bill asked. "Neither of us has a job, and you still have your student teaching to complete."

"We already have my apartment," Andrea replied, "and without your dorm fee our expenses would actually be less, wouldn't they?"

"Well, I guess so," he replied as he thought about the idea. "But I don't know if my dad would continue to pay my bills if I got married."

"We should be able to qualify for some grants if we're married," Andrea responded enthusiastically. "And besides, we'll have your student loans to help live on while you're in grad school."

The more Bill thought about the idea, the more it appealed to him. Graduation was only two months away, and then Andrea would be finished. They had planned to get married that next summer anyway and only have a simple ceremony with their families, so what difference would a couple of months make?

Besides, he thought, *Andrea's right. Her mother is certainly in no shape to go through a wedding.* "I think it's a great idea," he said as he put his arms around her. "When would you like to get married?"

"What about right now?" she said.

"Right now?" Bill echoed as he looked at his watch. "But it's nearly eleven o'clock, and we have classes tomorrow. Besides, we have to wait at least three days for the blood tests."

"We could miss Friday's classes," she argued, a little hurt that Bill was hesitating. "And we can always drive to Virginia—there's no waiting period and they don't require a blood test." Andrea's cousin had told her this, and she had verified the information on the Internet.

"But Andrea, that's nearly two hundred miles away. I don't even have gas money right now."

"I've got my credit cards," she responded eagerly. "It wouldn't cost that much, and we could stop down in Bristol on the way back and see my dad's sister. She's been wanting me to come and visit. It would be like a little honeymoon."

Bill had a nagging feeling inside about doing something this serious on impulse. He wondered what his parents, especially his mother, would say when she found out. But seeing Andrea so excited and knowing that they did love each other, he could come up with no logical arguments that would satisfy her. So he said, "Okay, Andrea, let's go for it. You pack some things, and I'll call my parents and let them know."

Andrea panicked inside as Bill mentioned calling his mom. "Please don't tell anyone right now," she pleaded. "They'll just try to talk us out of it. I want this to be our surprise. We'll tell them after graduation. Okay?"

Bill agreed reluctantly. He knew his mom would be hurt when she found out. Andrea said, "Let's just go like we are. We don't need any extra clothes. We'll only be gone two days at the most, and we can buy something if we really need it."

By this time Bill was totally into the idea as well, so he replied, "This is really crazy, but if that's what you want, we'll do it. At least we'll have something to tell our grandchildren."

Andrea grabbed Bill around the waist. "We're going to be so happy, Bill. I just know it."

Bill and Andrea took off for Virginia. Four hours later they stopped to eat a very late dinner. While they were eating, they mentioned to the motherly waitress that they were driving to Virginia to get married the next day.

"Do you have your license yet?" she asked.

"No," Bill replied. "We understand we don't have to wait in Virginia."

"Well, I don't know who told you that, honey," she said in a charming Southern drawl. "But it simply ain't true. You gotta wait at least two days."

"We can't wait," Andrea said in alarm. "We have to be back in school Monday morning."

"Well, I'd suggest you go to New Jersey then," the waitress said authoritatively. "You don't have to wait at all up there. That's where we got married a few years back."

"We can't drive all the way to New Jersey," Bill argued. "It would take ten or twelve more hours."

"But we can't just turn around and go back home," Andrea complained. "We've already come this far. Let's go on, please."

Bill was in no mood to discuss anything objectively, and when he saw the hurt on Andrea's face, he surrendered. "Okay," he said. "If you're willing, I am too. But let's get going. We'll just make it back in time."

Andrea had literally jumped out of her seat and was headed toward the door when Bill asked, "Do you have any cash, Andrea? I'm a little short to pay the bill."

Andrea dug into her purse and found about $3.00 in change. She asked the waitress, "Can I pay for the meal with my credit card?"

"Sorry," the waitress replied, "we don't take credit cards. The boss says they cost too much to process."

So Bill paid the check with what they could scrape together, and they headed toward New Jersey. Several hours later they entered New Jersey and encountered their first toll bridge. In the meantime, their periodic stops had exhausted their small cash reserve. The tollgate attendant told them that they would either have to pay the toll or turn around and go back.

"Can we pay the toll with a credit card?" Andrea asked.

"No, you can't, Miss," he answered. "Look, kids, the toll is only $1.10. Are you telling me you don't even have that much on you?"

Looking a little sheepish, Bill replied, "I'm afraid not. You see, we were planning to get married in Virginia, but when we found out we had to wait two days, we decided to drive up here instead. We have to be back in school Monday."

"Well, good luck. But I don't think you're getting off to a good start this way. Exactly how much do you have?"

"About fifty-six cents," Andrea said in a whisper.

"Tell you what I'll do," the attendant said in a stern voice. "Give me what you have, and I'll put in the difference. You're holding up traffic."

"Oh, thank you, sir," was Andrea's reply.

"Just one thing," the man said. "How are you planning to get back across?"

Bill was suddenly struck by the same thought. "How are we going to get back across with no money?"

"I have an aunt who lives just off the interstate," Andrea volunteered. "We'll go see her; it's just a few miles up. I'm sure she will help."

With a sinking feeling inside, Bill drove across the bridge and into New

Jersey. He realized that what they were doing didn't make any sense, but he didn't know what else to do. Andrea was totally committed to the idea of marriage. He was too, but he had some reservations about the timing. The thought crossed his mind that he was acting like a pushover.

They drove to Andrea's aunt's home. She was speechless when Andrea called her to say they were only a couple of miles away. But she asked them to come over and began to prepare some lunch.

When Andrea and Bill rang the doorbell, she opened it to find two worn-out and totally rumpled young people. "Andrea, come in," she said. "Who is your young man, and what in the world brings you here?"

"This is Bill, Aunt Maye," she said. "We're getting married and just dropped by to see you."

"Getting married?" Andrea's aunt said with surprise. "Does your mom know about this?"

"Well, no. She's really been depressed since Daddy's death, and we thought it would be better to elope and not put her through the stress of a wedding."

"Well, I can't argue that she's in no shape for any more emotional trauma," her aunt said. "But I don't know that running away to get married is the right answer. Do your parents know, Bill?"

"No, ma'am," he replied shyly. "But we are of legal age, and my folks know we plan to get married in the summer."

"Then why all the rush?" she asked.

Andrea jumped in with, "We just believe that's what God wants us to do, Aunt Maye. But we have a little problem and wondered if you could help."

"What kind of problem?"

"We've had to drive farther than we planned and ran out of cash. I wondered if you would mind cashing a small check for me."

"I don't want your check. I'll be glad to give you some money as a wedding present. But I certainly wish you would think about this some more."

"We have already thought about it, and we know this is what we want to do," Andrea said emphatically. Bill started to answer but changed his mind. Then Andrea's aunt said something that caught them off guard.

"But I don't understand why you drove all the way up here. New Jersey has a three-day waiting period before you can get married."

"That can't be," Andrea wailed. "The waitress said she got married here herself without a wait."

"That must have been some time ago then," her aunt said. "I'll check for you, but I'm sure that's right."

A quick look on the Internet confirmed her statement. "The closest place to get married with no wait is Virginia."

"That's impossible," Bill moaned. "We were just there and someone told us they had a waiting period too."

Another Internet check confirmed that they could get married without a wait if they were of legal age.

"I suspect the waitress thought you kids were not old enough to get married without permission," the aunt said. "Looks like you'll have to drive back to Virginia."

They decided to sleep a few hours before they headed back, and in the interim Andrea's aunt washed and dried their well-worn clothes. Four hours later they were back on the road, headed toward Virginia, where they finally found a justice of the peace who could issue the license and perform the ceremony. By that time they were totally broke and running out of time before classes started.

"That'll be twenty-five dollars," the justice said. "And thirty for the license."

"Will you take a credit card?" Andrea asked meekly.

"Sorry, ma'am, cash only," the justice responded brusquely.

"But we don't have any cash," Andrea pleaded. "Will you take a check?"

"I normally take cash only. It's Saturday night, and nobody can cash your check until Monday. You kids don't have any money at all?" he asked looking at Bill.

"No, sir," Bill replied.

"Well, I guess I'll have to take a check then," he said irritably, "but I'll need some collateral. I've been stiffed by too many of you college kids already."

"What kind of collateral?" Andrea asked nervously. She knew that if they didn't get a license, they weren't legally married.

"I'll take that watch you're wearing," he told Bill, pointing at his watch.

"But that's brand new," Andrea protested. "And it was a gift from me."

"Well, take it or leave it," the justice said gruffly. "Otherwise you can wait until Monday and cash your check at the bank."

"No, we can't wait," Bill said as he removed the watch. "Can we get it back after the check clears?"

"Why sure, kids. You just drop me a note, and I'll send it right along," he said with a chuckle.

❶ ❶ ❶

A month later Andrea's mother called her. "Andrea, I've been looking through some of the bills from my bank, and I see that the credit card is over limit. I called our banker, and he said he had let it overdraft because he knew about Daddy's death and figured I was waiting on the insurance payment. But Andrea, I haven't used that card much at all, and it has more than four thousand dollars charged on it."

"Four thousand dollars! Mother, that's impossible," Andrea explained. "I've used it for school expenses and some clothes, but I certainly didn't charge that much!"

"And the gas card has nearly eight hundred dollars on it too, Andrea. Have you used it? There are charges on here from Virginia, Washington, and New Jersey. Did you drive to New Jersey recently?"

Andrea sat quietly for a few seconds. She was overwhelmed by the news from her mother. She had put the trip and the charges completely out of her mind during the last month. Being married was everything to her, and she and Bill had been very happy. But now she knew she had to tell her mother that they were married. "Well, Mom, I've got some news. Bill and I got married a month ago in Virginia, but we also went up to see Aunt Maye in New Jersey. That's where the gas charges came from. But don't worry, we'll pay you back."

Andrea's mother had already put two and two together and suspected something like that. After a moment she said, "That was your choice, but I wish you had at least let me know before you got married. I wish you had told me. Do Bill's parents know? They'll probably be upset if you left them out of this too, but you'll have to work that out for yourselves. You know I wish you and Bill all the best. And since your dad and I always said that when you got married you would have to manage your own household, I'm sending all the bills to you. You'll have to take care of them."

"But Mom," she pleaded, "we don't have the money to pay all the bills right now. I'm student teaching, and Bill is getting ready for his finals next month."

"I'm sorry, Andrea, but you should have considered that before you got married and ran up those bills." With that, she hung up the phone.

Andrea looked around the small room that served as their living area. There sat the television and stereo she had charged on the credit card before she and Bill were married, and she realized that she probably *had* charged four thousand dollars—and more. She had been using the card since they got married and was frightened as she realized that they may well have charged another several hundred dollars. Graduation was still five weeks away, and without income they would have no way to make payments on their credit card bill. She decided not to tell Bill anything about what her mother had said until after graduation. He needed to concentrate on end-of-semester matters, and she knew he would worry himself sick about the bills. He already looked haggard from concern over what he would tell his parents.

For nearly two weeks Andrea tried diligently not to use the credit card for anything. Her mother had sent her the bills, and after looking through them, she knew they were her charges. Then one evening while Bill was in a class, she got a call on her cell phone from Bill's mother.

"Andrea, I'm trying to find Bill. Is he with you?" she asked.

Without thinking, Andrea replied, "No, he's still in class. He'll be home later this afternoon."

There was a long pause on the other end of the line. Andrea tried to think of something to say, but decided that this was as good a time as any for Bill's mother to find out.

"Are you and Bill living together?" Bill's mother asked with a measured calmness.

"Well, Mrs. Yates, we have good news for you! We got married about a month ago," Andrea replied. "I know we should have told you both right away, but, well . . . we decided so fast, and—we've both been so busy," she finished lamely.

"We knew something was going on when the school e-mailed and told us Bill had moved out of the dorm," she said sternly. "I do think you both owed us enough respect to tell us yourselves. But if you're married, you're married. Please tell Bill to call me when he comes in. We would like for you both to come down for a day as soon as you can."

"We will, I promise," Andrea replied. "And we're very happy, Mrs. Yates. We do love each other, and we didn't do this to hurt anyone."

"Andrea, you're a member of our family now, and we love you too. But you both need to learn that God wants us to be honest about everything. I'm disappointed that you didn't trust us enough to let us in on your decision. You can't start a relationship with an attitude of distrust. Please remember that in your marriage too."

When they hung up Andrea sat still for several minutes. What Bill's mother had said hit her in a sensitive spot. She knew they had been deceitful to their parents, and she knew she had been deceiving Bill. It had gone on so long now she was wondering how he would react when he finally knew the whole truth. When Bill came home, she told him about his mother's call.

He looked like he was going to be sick for a minute. Then he said, "I don't blame her for being hurt and angry. I know I've been lying to them since we got married. I'd better call her and at least let her know I'm sorry."

"I'm sorry, Bill," Andrea said honestly. "I suppose I'm the one at fault. You wanted to call her, and I talked you out of it. I was afraid she would convince you not to get married."

"No, Andrea, I'm the one at fault. I know I'm supposed to be responsible. If I had had the courage, I would have been honest with my parents up front. I just hope this doesn't affect our relationship with them from now on."

After a brief conversation with his mother and his father, Bill hung up the phone. "Well, they're both hurt," he said. "But they want you to know that they're glad to have you as a member of our family, and they've accepted the situation. My dad said that we'll have to come up with the money for grad school ourselves. He believes we should stand on our own two feet. I guess that means I'll have to put it off for a while — at least until we can save a little money."

"What about graduation expenses and the school loans?" Andrea asked apprehensively. She had intended to tell Bill about the other debts, but now she wondered if she should.

"He said he'll continue to pay until I graduate, and they're going to give us two thousand dollars as a wedding gift to help us get started. The school loans are mine to pay, but I knew that from the beginning."

Andrea decided she would wait to tell Bill about the debts until he had a chance to recover from the shock of telling his parents. The opportunity didn't come up again before graduation, and with the wedding money from Bill's parents they were able to get by for the next month.

Bill found a job as a cashier in a music store. Although it didn't pay much, he figured he could find something better after the summer break, when all the other students went back to school.

One evening Bill answered the doorbell, and there stood Andrea's mother. "Mrs. Carlisle, come in. What a nice surprise!" he said.

"Bill, I need to talk with you and Andrea about something urgent. Is she here?"

"Yes, she is," he replied. At that moment Andrea came around the door from the bedroom saying, "Who's at the door, Bill?" When she saw her mother, she paled.

"Mother, what are you doing here?" she asked in a hollow voice.

"Andrea, you know very well what I'm doing here," her mother answered. "It's about these." With that, she thrust a handful of credit card receipts in front of her. "You told me you were going to take care of these, and now I have received notice that the bank is filing suit against me."

"What are those?" Bill asked as Andrea made her way back to the living room couch.

"They're credit card bills," Andrea's mother said in an accusing tone. "Didn't Andrea tell you I called her about them nearly two months ago?"

Bill looked over at Andrea. One glance told him the answer. "No, she didn't," he said. "But if they're our bills, I give you my word we'll pay every one of them, Mrs. Carlisle."

"Well, I hope you will," she replied as she headed for the door again. "I want you both to know how disappointed I am that you started out this way. It's partly my fault, too. Apparently we didn't teach Andrea some things she needed to know, especially about handling money. We never had very much ourselves and always lived on what little we had. I guess we just assumed our daughter would know how to do the same." With that she walked over to Andrea, who was crying softly, and hugged her.

"You know I love you—you too, Bill— but you need to grow up. There are responsibilities that come with being an adult. I can't pay these bills, but I wouldn't even if I could. You need to accept the consequences of your actions. And you need to be totally honest with your husband," she said in a solemn tone.

After Andrea's mother left, Bill sat down to talk with her about the bills. "How much do we really owe, Andrea?" he asked, his voice controlled.

"I don't know," she replied. "I haven't added up all the bills yet. I'm sorry for not telling you before. I didn't want to bother you during your finals, and then I was afraid to tell you."

"Andrea, you don't need to be afraid to tell me anything. But we do need to figure out exactly how much we owe and how we're going to pay."

After two hours of poring over the bills that had come in and estimating those that had not been sent yet, Bill came up with a figure of nearly five thousand dollars between the gas card and the bank card.

"What are we going to do?" Andrea asked Bill.

"I don't know right now," he answered. "But grad school is out for the fall. And I'm going to need to look for a better job, or we'll be going further in the hole each month."

"I can get a job, too," Andrea offered. "I complete my internship in a little more than a week. But school doesn't start again for nearly three months, so I won't know about a teaching job for a month or more."

"Andrea, we're both going to have to make some sacrifices to pay these debts," Bill said. "I've really been foolish not to see that we were living over our heads. I guess I didn't want to know. I'm going to Pastor Riggs tomorrow to see if he knows anyone who can help us work out a plan."

The next day Bill stopped by to see his pastor and told him the overview of what had happened. "Unfortunately, Bill, what has happened to you and Andrea is not unusual today. Too much credit is put in the hands of young people who have little or no idea how to control their use of it. I'm sure Andrea was as shocked as her mother to find out how much she had spent."

"There's no question about that, Pastor," Bill responded. "But I need to know what we can do about it. We'll pay back everything in time, but right now it looks kind of hopeless."

"It's never hopeless if you're willing to admit your mistakes and correct them," the pastor commented. "I want you to call one of our elders who heads up our financial coaching program. He'll work out a time to meet with you and Andrea."

Bill immediately called Mike McKenna, the elder Pastor Riggs referred him to. "I'll be glad to see you and Andrea this evening, Bill. I'll meet you at the church office at seven o'clock, if that's okay with you."

"That will be fine," Bill responded. "And thank you for taking the time."

"Don't mention it. That's my area of ministry to our fellowship. See you tonight at seven."

At seven o'clock Bill and Andrea were waiting outside the church office. Mike McKenna arrived, and Bill recognized him from a meeting he had attended more than a year ago, when the elder had spoken on the need to be good managers of the material things God has provided. *I sure wish I had listened better*, Bill said to himself.

Bill and Andrea described the events of the past several months that had brought them to the point where they were. Mike made several notes as they discussed the particular events.

"As I see it," he said, "you have several symptoms and two basic problems."

"What do you mean?" Andrea asked. "What's the difference?"

"The problems created the symptoms," he responded. "For instance, you now owe nearly five thousand dollars in consumer debt. But that's a symptom of a much deeper problem, I believe. If your parents just gave you the money to pay the bills, I believe they would be doing you a disservice, because it's likely that you would repeat the same mistakes again."

"Not me," Andrea said emphatically.

"I know that's what you think right now," he said. "And probably you wouldn't repeat the exact same mistakes. But indulgence comes in many forms, and future mistakes can create much more severe consequences. I've seen people who make more than $150,000 a year get deeply into debt because their impulses grew even faster than their salaries.

"I think I can help you get out from under the circumstances, if you're willing to sacrifice for a while. But unless you recognize the problems and solve them, you'll be back again."

"What do you think the problems are?" Bill asked.

"As I see it, Bill, your problem stems from a lack of self-confidence. But it shows itself in the fact that you haven't accepted your responsibility as the head of your family."

"What do you mean?"

"First you allowed yourself to be talked into a quick elopement, and because you didn't want to hurt Andrea's feelings, you weren't honest with her. No sound relationship can ever be built on a foundation of fear. Remember what the Bible teaches us: perfect love casts out all fear."

"But I don't want to dictate to Andrea," Bill argued. However, even as he said it, he knew somewhere deep inside that what Mike had said was right. He did fear losing Andrea, and that was his prime motivation the weekend they eloped. He had seen the foolishness of what they were doing even from the beginning, but he didn't have the courage to tell her no.

"I don't mean that you should dictate to your wife, Bill. She is to be your equal partner. But you must accept that God's plan for the husband is for him to take responsibility for his family—not follow his wife as if on a leash. That hasn't happened with you yet, but it will if you allow it. Andrea has the stronger personality and will tend to set the pace."

"Wait a minute. You're making me sound like I want to wear the pants in the family," Andrea protested.

"I don't believe you do, Andrea. But you need to realize that you have a more dominant personality and that you must learn to control it."

"Is that the second problem then?" she asked meekly.

"No, the second problem you need to deal with is your extravagant attitude toward money," Mike said bluntly.

"What do you mean?" Andrea objected. "I don't think I'm extravagant. I've never wasted money before this."

"But Andrea, you never had the opportunity before," Mike replied. "From what you said, I suspect that your dad ran your home and doled out the money he wanted you to have. And he was probably pretty cautious with his money, wasn't he?"

"Well, yeah," Andrea agreed. "But I never thought of myself as extravagant."

"Some of the spending was ignorance about credit cards. But when the totals come to five thousand dollars, it usually goes far beyond just simple ignorance," Mr. McKenna said. "Some people have such a—well, a lack of self-control—that they cannot pass by anything they don't already have. It's almost an obsession. Often it's not even for themselves. They will even buy gifts for other people and charge them on their credit cards."

Andrea thought about the watch she had bought Bill. She had bought him another one two weeks after they returned home. Bill had protested, but she'd convinced him to keep it.

Mike continued, "We all like to buy things, and we can all indulge, given the opportunity and the resources. But some people are what I would call shop-a-holics. They feel best when they're buying something, even if they know they can't afford it."

Andrea realized that much of what the coach was saying did apply to her. She never had splurged very much, but she hadn't had the opportunity until she had her mother's credit card. Then it became a need that she had to satisfy. She had felt the same way about getting married that weekend. She didn't think she was going to lose Bill, but she wasn't willing to take the chance.

"Does that mean I should never handle the money again?" Andrea asked dejectedly.

"Not at all. It just means that you need to realize that Bill is in your life to offset your imbalances, just as you are to offset his. When you recognize what those imbalances are and learn to communicate about them openly, you'll be further along than 90 percent of couples today. I'll give you some homework to do together to help you better understand God's plan for your marriage and your finances.

"In the meantime we need to deal with the immediate problem—these debts. I notice in your list of assets that you own two cars. Is that right?"

"Right," Bill said. "Andrea's and mine."

"How much do you think they're worth?"

"I would say mine is worth close to two thousand at best, and Andrea's a little less," Bill replied.

"And I see that you have a stereo and television. Anything else of any substantial value, like an insurance policy or stocks?"

"No," Bill replied again, "just the normal junk furniture that most college students accumulate over the years."

"Bill, I do have a small insurance policy that Daddy bought for me when I was a little girl," Andrea said.

"Do you know if it has any cash value, Andrea?" Mr. McKenna asked.

"I think so. I had forgotten that I even had it until you mentioned the insurance. Daddy said it would pay either a lump sum or provide enough for burial, but I don't know how much."

"Okay, what we have to work with, then, is the potential sale of one car, a stereo, a TV, and some cash in an insurance policy."

"But we need both of our cars if we're both going to work," Andrea argued. "Bill works on the west end of town, and as soon as I finish my student teaching, I'll probably have a job in another."

"I know it won't be easy, but it is possible. You both need to be totally realistic about your situation, and since we don't have a lot of leeway in time, I'm going to lay it out for you. I hope this doesn't frighten you, but you need to face reality.

"First, the bank has already started action against Andrea's mother. In less than two weeks, there will be a court hearing, and I feel sure the judge will grant the petition to attach her property unless we can work out another arrangement in the meantime.

"Second, even without the debts, you're living beyond your means right now. You can't afford a second car. It takes extra insurance, maintenance, and gas.

"Third, I assume that the stereo and TV were bought with the credit card, so you need to sell them and return the money to the bank. Obviously you won't get back what you paid, but that's the way it is usually.

"Even after you do these things, your budget won't balance while you're paying off the remaining debts, unless you both work. That means you have another choice to make. Andrea, you will have to find a job as soon as possible, and, Bill, you'll have to find another job with a more stable income."

"We already decided to do that," Bill offered. "And I realize that I won't be able to go to grad school in the fall."

"Not necessarily," Mr. McKenna said. "If you could live with one set of parents and go to school closer to home, it might be possible to at least start evening classes."

"I don't know about that," Bill said. "I think both of our parents are peeved at us right now."

"Do you really blame them?" Mike asked. "So far, you've gotten married on an impulse, failed to tell the people who love you the most, charged five thousand dollars on someone else's credit card, and a bank in your hometown is ready to sue Andrea's mother."

"I guess when you look at it that way, we don't come out looking too good," Andrea said.

"But it's not too late to change," the elder assured them. "Now it's time to start doing things God's way."

"What do you mean?" Bill asked.

"First, sell whatever you don't actually need to live on, and give the money to your creditors. Look." He read Proverbs 3:27–28 to them: "Do not withhold good from those who deserve it, when it is in your power to act. Do not say to your neighbor, 'Come back later; I'll give it tomorrow'—when you now have it with you."

"Next, contact your creditors and ask their forgiveness. Then work out a repayment plan with them.

"And learn to think and plan before you act. Jesus said, 'Suppose one of you wants to build a tower. Will he not first sit down and estimate the cost to see if he has enough money to complete it? For if he lays the foundation and is not able to finish it, everyone who sees it will ridicule him.' That's from

Luke 14, if you'd like to look it up and read it for yourselves later. So from this point on, you both need to vow that you won't make impetuous decisions and that you will pray about every decision and discuss it thoroughly.

"Andrea, you have been blessed with an ability to lead and direct. Those qualities will be very beneficial both in your career and in the home. But you must be willing to listen and let Bill be a man. God promises to guide your decisions, but you need to operate as a team and expect Bill to take responsibility.

"Now I'd like for you both to contact the bank and the credit manager for the gas company and work out a repayment plan. Tell them you're in the process of selling some assets and will pay them that money up front. Feel free to tell them you're working with me. They can e-mail me for verification. And one more thing: I'll do everything I can to help you get out of this situation, but you must agree to develop a budget together and stick to it diligently during this process. If not, I'd be better off to spend my time with those who are willing to listen."

"Okay, that all sounds doable. We'll stick to the plan. I want to get out of this mess and get our lives back on track," Bill said.

"And how about you, Andrea?" asked Mike.

"Same here," Andrea responded, "but I'm really afraid that what you said about my being an impulse spender is true. What if I can't control myself and do this again?"

"Andrea, spending is not like alcoholism or drug addiction, although it can be if you don't exercise self-control. You need to establish some guidelines for yourself that include relying on Bill to balance your extremes. Once you make a budget, don't violate it. That doesn't mean you can't ever spend any money or that you won't need some money just for your own use. Everybody does. But limit yourself to what you can afford, and don't rely on credit cards to fill in the gaps. Credit makes it too easy to splurge and is too difficult to pay back. If you stick to your repayment plan, you should be out of debt in a short while. Remember, too, that a lot of tension in marriage is from money, and you want to see your marriage start out on a good footing."

"I do," Bill said. "We both do. I don't know what we would have done if it weren't for your help. I really was beginning to feel the pressure."

"I haven't done anything but help you realize that there's an answer to your problems. Now it's up to you to work out the details and stick to them. I'll give you some materials that will help you understand the basic principles from God's Word. These must be your guide if you want to make good decisions in the future. You need to learn how to keep your accounts accurately and keep up with your monthly budget. We'll work that out together over the next few weeks."

Bill and Andrea called the vice president of the bank in charge of credit card accounts and asked for a meeting the next day. They told him exactly what had happened and asked if there were a way they could work out a repayment plan. He agreed to convert the credit card debt into a personal loan, collateralized by both of their cars. The next month Bill's car was sold, and they were able to pay the money they received toward the loan amount.

Andrea sold the stereo and television and used that money to pay on the loan. Within a few weeks they had the loan amount down to less than $2,600. They worked out a repayment plan with the gas company with the help of Mike McKenna, so they could pay the minimum amount until the bank loan was repaid. The cash from the insurance policy reduced the loan by another $780.

Bill took a job with a national delivery service that paid nearly twice what he had been making. Andrea took a job in telephone sales and found that she really enjoyed the work. Between the two of them, they were able to pay off the bank loan in five months, although it meant a lot of scrimping and early mornings as Bill would drop Andrea off at her job and then drive across town to his. But after three months, Bill's employer allowed him to drive the company delivery van home in the evenings. That not only provided them a second vehicle, nearly cost-free, but also lowered their gas bill considerably.

In the fall, Andrea accepted a teaching position with a private school, and they began to settle into a reasonably normal routine. Over the course of three months they counseled with Mike McKenna once a week. During that time they learned how to balance and maintain their checking account and how to develop a realistic budget. In the fourth month Mr. McKenna called Bill to ask if he and Andrea would be willing to meet and coach another young couple the pastor had sent to him. Bill asked Andrea, who wholeheartedly agreed, and they began their first one-on-one coaching to help another couple.

Bill ultimately finished his master's work and went on to get a PhD in music. He now heads a department at the university where he and Andrea attended school. They lived with Andrea's mother for about a year and a half, during which time they helped her get started on a budget. During that time Andrea's mother also trained for her new career in practical nursing, which she could afford to do only because of their financial assistance for nearly four years. Bill and Andrea's financial recovery was possible only because they faced their problems honestly and worked through them together.

INTERLUDE

A Quick History Lesson

The Bible Speaks on Debt and Borrowing

Common Debt Traps

A QUICK HISTORY LESSON

D_{ebt.}

Nothing in the area of finances has so dominated or influenced the direction of our society during the last few decades as much as debt. It's amazing when you consider that credit cards have only played an influential role in American life since the 1980s.[1] It was once unusual to finance a car purchase, and mortgages used to be mostly for GIs who were getting their starter homes. But today, it is typical for the American household's debt to include credit cards, car loan(s), and a mortgage. Often the list extends even farther to include consolidation loans, finance company loans, and parental loans.

And education? Students with an undergrad college degree carry an average debt of $21,000 in student loans.[2] Even graduates of professional or vocational programs complete their training with an average student loan debt of $10,000.[3]

How did our culture change so quickly? A look back will help us understand how the cycle of debt and credit became part of our way of life.

The Great Depression (from 1929 until the start of World War II) made a lasting impact on millions of people who lost a lifetime of earnings in re-possessed farms and mortgages. It also left a lasting impact on lenders, who found themselves in the position of having to repossess homes and farms that were virtually worthless to them. The Depression forced Americans to conserve again. Bankers began to make loans only with adequate collateral, and borrowers were extremely cautious because they realized the risks.

But after the Second World War, the government found itself with several million ex-GIs who needed homes, jobs, and educations. With the aftermath of the Great Depression still fresh in their minds, commercial lenders, such as banks, and savings and loans, were reluctant to extend credit to so many men who had virtually no credit history. So, as a last resort, the government became the lender. Congress passed laws allowing the federal government to guarantee loans made to ex-servicemen, and the GI Bill was born. This law allowed commercial lenders to extend credit for education and housing to millions of wartime veterans, and it provided government guarantees to back those loans.

The impact on the economy was immediate and spectacular. Millions of Americans went to college, and millions more borrowed money to build homes and start businesses. The great credit boom of the twentieth century was off and running. Never before in history had our government used tax-generated dollars to support private lending, but the American people supported the idea wholeheartedly and a new idea was born: consumer credit. Soon the government programs were expanded to provide government backed loans to nonveterans through the Federal Housing Administration, the Federal Farm Loan Administration, the Small Business Administration, and so on.

With the stimulus of credit feeding the education, housing, and business sectors, prices went up—the natural outgrowth of the law of supply and demand. Credit allowed more people to compete for the available products and services, which in turn allowed prices to increase. Once the cycle began, others were forced to borrow to compete for those items, and private lenders stepped in to provide the loans. The boom of home loans in the 1950s provided better housing to young couples at a much earlier age than they ever could have realized by saving to buy their homes.

But there was a price to be paid, and that price was inflation. Home prices began to creep up in the late 1950s, as more and more families entered the market through a wide variety of mortgage options. But as prices climbed, many couples were forced out of the market because they could not afford the monthly payments. The bankers, still leaning toward the conservative side, applied the 25 percent rule to housing loans, meaning that no more than 25 percent of the husband's total monthly income could be dedicated to home mortgage payments.

The impasse created by that policy led to a slowdown in buying, not only in the housing industry but also in related industries, such as appliances, carpeting, and real estate. A parallel predicament was evident in the automobile industry and in education, both of which had become heavily dependent on consumers' use of loans to buy their products and services. The answer came in the form of longer-term loans. By extending the payment period, lenders enabled people with relatively low incomes to afford the monthly payments. Another boom was on.

By the mid-60s, the generation of bankers who had been through the Great Depression was retiring and turning operations over to younger, more aggressive people who had grown up with the debt-oriented mentality. The need to expand the credit base meant that even more loans had to be made available to more people for longer periods of time.

By the 1970s, virtually every segment of the economy was dependent on credit. Even consumer items like food, clothing, medical care, and travel were dependent on credit through credit cards and small loans. Lenders extended long-term loans based on equity in assets. Thus consumers could borrow on the appreciated values of their homes, stocks, and businesses. But since the equity was dependent on the availability of loans to subsequent buyers, this created the need for even more lending. The economy was returning to the pre-Depression mentality of growth through debt.

In the 1970s, the government was no longer just the guarantor of loans. It was the stimulator of massive debt. The economy had become totally dependent on consumers' borrowing to keep it going. The traditional requirements for qualifying borrowers fell by the wayside as lenders sought wider markets for their loans. No longer was the rule in mortgage loans 25 percent of the husband's salary. Now it was 40 percent of both incomes. Car loans were extended to sixty months and often had balloon payments of up to 40 percent at the completion of the loan period.

By the 80s and 90s, debt had become the engine that fueled the entire economy, and consumers were forced to borrow even the equity out of their homes in order to educate their children and purchase cars. In the 90s, leasing automobiles, previously a practice for businesses only, almost became a way of life. Is it any wonder that in the midst of this steamroller of debt financing the average family experienced financial problems?

The problem of personal debt only worsened in the decade following 2000. Under the Community Reinvestment Act, the federal government had begun to pressure banks into making sub-prime housing loans in the 1990s. That pressure, coupled with an implicit understanding that the federal government would underwrite risky, sub-prime loans, caused an epidemic of personal debt to break out across America. Mortgages totaling hundreds of billions of dollars were handed out to low-income (or no-income) individuals who had no means of repaying them.[4]

Government sponsored enterprises such as the Federal National Mortgage Association (Fannie Mae) and the Federal Home Loan Mortgage Corporation (Freddie Mac) had for years masked the problem by buying up this "bad paper," but the bill came due in September 2008 as the federal government was forced to directly take over Fannie Mae and Freddie Mac, placing the bankrupt corporations into "conservatorship,"[5] and putting taxpayers on the hook for hundreds of billions of dollars.

The dramatic increase in mortgage accessibility and increasing consumer spending caused American household debt to nearly double between 2000 and 2007, eventually reaching a record $13.8 *trillion*.[6]

If the 2008 "Great Recession" had a silver lining, it was that the high rate of foreclosures and the fear of job loss led many Americans to dramatically increase their saving[7] and reduce consumer debt[8] as the first decade of the new millennium drew to a close.

The BIBLE SPEAKS on DEBT and BORROWING

It's time to discuss principles from the Bible concerning debt and borrowing, because much of the counsel on these topics in this book is based on those principles.

BIBLICAL PRINCIPLES OF DEBT

1: Debtors are in servitude to the one who lends to them

Debt is not a well-understood term today. Most people use the word *debt* to describe any borrowing, but, although that is not entirely inaccurate, it is not precise enough.

Scripture goes beyond that definition to describe the conditions of indebtedness. Even if a debt is current (all payments up to date), the borrower is potentially in a position of servitude. "The rich rule over the poor, and the borrower is servant to the lender" (Proverbs 22:7). But if the debt is delinquent, the lender is given an implied authority from God, according to the Bible.

In the time of Christ that authority extended to imprisonment, slavery, and the confiscation of a borrower's total worldly possessions. Not once in

Scripture is there even a hint that that was not the legitimate right of a lender. The only variable that Scripture allows is that, if the lender and the borrower were both Jews, the borrower would be released from servitude at the end of seven years, unless that person voluntarily elected to remain a slave. To say the least, borrowing was not a decision to be taken lightly.

The same basic rules applied in America even in the twentieth century. Almost any major city still has in its library records from a debtors' prison. I found several good examples from the turn of the century in Atlanta. One record read, "Abraham Johnston, white male, commended to debtors' prison for a period of six years, or until the debt is resolved, for failure to pay the agreed-upon sum of two hundred dollars for the purchase of a mule."

Another read, "Sara Wright is sentenced to debtors' prison for an indefinite period of time for habitual indebtedness." The sentence went on to describe her despicable crimes, such as charging food that she couldn't pay for at a merchant's store, charging dry goods at a department store, and signing for a loan with a local citizen without the ability to make restitution.

It is evident that our attitudes today about debt and those of our predecessors were somewhat different. The cause for the difference can be pinpointed as greed and indulgence. Not on the part of the borrowers—that came later. The initial greed was on the part of elected officials who desired to expand our economy by way of debt. To do so required a drastic alteration of the rules regarding borrowing and the consequences of a failure to repay.

Few people today are willing to risk forfeiting their freedom and separation from their families to borrow money. The risk would simply be too great. So the laws were amended to make borrowing less risky and credit more available. And besides, who would tolerate the government borrowing massive amounts of money that could not be repaid, while friends and relatives languished in debtors' prisons for failure to repay their personal loans?

The old laws for delinquent debts seem harsh and unnecessarily cruel to us today, and perhaps they were. But the principles behind them were sound and just. The laws assumed that nobody was forced to borrow money;

they borrowed money voluntarily. The lender extended honor (money), and the borrower represented himself as trustworthy. Thus the punishment for defaulting on a debt was actually more severe than for theft because it was considered a breach of trust.

2: Borrowing is permitted in Scripture

Many books have been written about handling money from a biblical viewpoint, many seminars have been taught, and there is no shortage of websites for reference. Some well-intentioned Christian teachers have taken the position that all borrowing is prohibited according to God's Word and that, consequently, Christians should not be involved in any borrowing or lending. Almost without exception, the biblical reference such teachers use to support their position is, "Let no debt remain outstanding, except the continuing debt to love one another, for he who loves his fellowman has fulfilled the law" (Romans 13:8).

I wish it were that simple, but it isn't. When I first came across Romans 13:8 in my study on finances, I thought, "Aha! Here is the justification for telling Christians to get rid of all credit, especially Christians who have misused it." But then I found myself in a quandary. If God, through the apostle Paul, intended to tell His people that all borrowing was prohibited, why are there New Testament Scriptures instructing men to repay what they borrow? That would be like prohibiting theft and then giving detailed instructions in how to invest stolen money. Obviously, that's ridiculous, which is why in the Bible you don't find principles regarding the handling of stolen goods.

Of course, God may have decided that it was time for His people to become totally debt-free, and thus in the New Testament changed the rules that had previously held true concerning indebtedness. But only those two alternatives exist: Either God changed the rules for His people and we had better get about the business of eliminating debt immediately, or Romans 13:8 doesn't mean that Christians should never borrow anything.

So I did some evaluation of the passage in Romans. I'd like to share my conclusions, because I believe they are accurate and confirmed by the pre-ponderance of Scripture. You can read the same passages and make up your own mind. Just bear in mind that when I began my study I was looking for a justification of the teaching that all borrowing is unscriptural.

To understand Romans 13:8, it is necessary to go back to Romans 13:6, where Paul discusses the payment of taxes. Christians in Paul's day often took the position that they should not have to pay taxes to the government of Rome because it was a heathen government. Paul admonished the believ-ers, saying that as Roman subjects they were to obey the laws regarding taxes. I'm sure that when he did this, he was keeping in mind the Lord's discussion of taxes in Matthew 22:17–21 and that he believed that it was unscriptural for Christians to refuse to pay their taxes. Paul expanded and restated his instructions concerning the payment of taxes: "Give everyone what you owe him: If you owe taxes, pay taxes; if revenue, then revenue; if respect, then respect; if honor, then honor" (Romans 13:7).

With the background of verses 6 and 7 in mind, in Paul's directive to Christians to "let no debt remain outstanding," "no debt" takes on a different significance than it might if it were read in isolation. Paul was summing up the legally prescribed duty all men had to pay their taxes and to respect gov-ernment officials. He was not giving a new teaching on the subject of bor-rowing money but, rather, was reconfirming a previous admonition to obey the law. Thus we can say that although borrowing is not promoted scriptur-ally, it is not prohibited.

BIBLICAL PRINCIPLES OF BORROWING

Principles of borrowing appear in God's Word, although it needs to be re-membered that these are principles, not laws. From time to time an overzeal-ous teacher will present principles as if they were laws. They are not. A prin-ciple is an instruction from the Lord to help guide our decisions. A law is an absolute. Negative consequences may follow from ignoring a principle, but punishment is the likely consequence of ignoring a law God has given us.

An example from our society is drinking and driving. A good guideline, or principle, to follow is never to drink. But the law says that if you drink and drive, you can lose your license and perhaps go to jail.

The principle of borrowing given in Scripture is that it is better not to provide security for a loan. "A man lacking in judgment strikes hands in pledge and puts up security for his neighbor" (Proverbs 17:18). If your neighbor—or friend or family member—is unable to pay the debt, you are responsible for it.

The law of borrowing given in Scripture is that it is a sin to borrow and not repay. "The wicked borrow and do not repay, but the righteous give generously" (Psalm 37:21). The assumption in the verse is that the wicked person can repay but will not, as opposed to an individual who wants to repay but cannot.

Principles are given to keep us clearly within God's path so that we can experience His blessings. To ignore them puts us in a constant state of jeopardy in which Satan can cause us to stumble at any time.

1: Debt is not the norm

Regardless of how it seems today, debt is not the norm in any economy and should not be the norm for God's people. We live in a debt-ridden society that is now virtually dependent on a constant expansion of credit to keep the economy going. That is a symptom of a society no longer willing to follow God's principles. We see this disobedience in many areas, so why should we assume it is any different in the area of money? Yet Christians who would never think of actively participating in a lifestyle of sinful behavior naively follow the world's path in the area of credit.

Listen to the promise God made His people: "If you fully obey the Lord your God and carefully follow all his commands I give you today, the Lord your God will set you high above all the nations on earth. . . . The Lord will open the heavens, the storehouse of his bounty, to send rain on your land in season and to bless all the work of your hands. You will lend to many nations *but will borrow from none*" (Deuteronomy 28:1, 12, emphasis added).

2: *Do not accumulate long-term debt*

It's hard to believe that a typical American family accepts a thirty-year home mortgage as normal today.

Some experts advise choosing a thirty-year mortgage over a fifteen-year loan, since the payments will most likely be lower. The thinking is that you can use any excess funds to pay down the principal.

Consider a house that was purchased for $225,000 with a down payment of $10,000, making the amount financed $215,000. At a rate of 4.625 percent, the payment on a thirty-year loan would be $1,105.

The same house with a fifteen-year mortgage would carry a monthly payment of $1,631, a clear difference.

However, on the fifteen-year loan, the payment breaks down to $847.15 in principal and $783.85 in interest. But in the thirty-year arrangement, only $276.74 goes toward the principal—the remaining $828.65 of the payment is interest.

Halfway into the loan, the buyer with the fifteen-year loan is putting far more into principal than interest. But for the buyer with the thirty-year loan, halfway is fifteen years, and at this point, $316.63 is going toward principal and $788.37 toward interest—and interest is just money thrown away.[1]

Obviously, house prices and interest rates fluctuate regionally and with the economy. The figures in the example above are just to show how long-term debt might look attractive today, but will really cost far more when added up over the years. If possible, it's better to have a shorter time to pay off what you owe than to become obligated to a long-term debt.

But what is that average home really worth? To determine that, assume that homes could no longer be sold using long-term mortgages. How much would the average home sell for if it could be bought with cash only? It would begin to sell for tens of thousands of dollars less. The additional cost is inflation, created through the use of long-term debt.

The longest term of debt God's people took on in the Bible was about seven years. During the year of remission (the seventh year) the Jew was instructed to release his brother from any indebtedness. "At the end of every seven years you must cancel debts. This is how it is to be done: Every creditor shall cancel the loan he has made to his fellow Israelite. He shall not require payment from his fellow Israelite or brother, because the Lord's time for canceling debts has been proclaimed" (Deuteronomy 15:1–2). Thus, the only debts that could exceed seven years were those made to non-Jews or from non-Jews.

3: Avoid surety

Surety is "a pledge or promise made to secure against loss, damage, or default; a security."[2]

The only way to avoid surety is to collateralize a loan with property that will cover the indebtedness, no matter what. Many home buyers think that because they buy an appreciating asset, such as a home, they are safe from surety, but that is not so. In most states a lender can sue to collect a deficit on a home mortgage in the event of a default. And remember that most defaults happen during a bad economy, when the prices of homes are most likely to drop, as was the case in the recession of 2008–2009.

Credit card purchases have become the most common form of surety in our generation. In this transaction one merchant sells you the material, and another finances the purchase (except for in-store credit cards). In the event of a default, the return of the merchandise does not cancel the debt, because the finance company has no interest in the merchandise.

Another meaning of surety is "One contracted to be responsible for another, especially one who assumes responsibilities or debts in the event of default."[3] The most recognizable form of surety is cosigning for the loan of another person.

4: The borrower has an absolute commitment to repay

In our society, situational ethics are widely accepted, so it is easy to rationalize not paying a debt, especially when the product or service is defective or when one's financial situation seems to be out of control. In the 1990s and during the first five years of the twenty-first century, easy access to credit led many people to believe that paying their debts would be a snap. Unfortunately, many borrowers discovered that it was possible for them to accumulate far more debt than they could repay and still maintain the lifestyle they wanted. As a result, they bailed out.

For example, in 1999, about 1,500,000 people chose personal, non-business bankruptcy as a way to avoid repayment. Yet the average indebtedness for couples in bankruptcy was only about $6,300. Due to changes in the bankruptcy law in 2005, it is not as easy to file for bankruptcy today. Still, people who are getting in over their heads may continue overspending, believing that somehow they will qualify for bankruptcy.

You may even hear some Christian teachers draw a parallel between modern law on bankruptcy and the year of jubilee prescribed by God: "Consecrate the fiftieth year and proclaim liberty throughout the land to all its inhabitants. It shall be a jubilee for you; each one of you is to return to his family property, and each to his own clan" (Leviticus 25:10).

I wish I could support the view that the year of jubilee and voluntary bankruptcy are comparable, but they aren't. Voluntary bankruptcy is an act by a borrower to avoid his or her creditors. The year of jubilee (as well as the year of remission) was a voluntary act by a lender to forgive indebtedness—a significant difference.

In some situations a voluntary bankruptcy is acceptable, but only in the context of trying to protect the creditors—never in the context of trying to avoid repayment.

Christians need to accept the hard truth that God allows them no alternative to keeping vows. That is why the Bible warns us to be careful before making vows. "It is better not to vow than to make a vow and not fulfill it" (Ecclesiastes 5:5).

COMMON DEBT TRAPS

As our look at the people in our stories has demonstrated, a common thread in most of their experiences was the lack of thorough planning. Sometimes this flaw is amplified by ignorance, imprudence, or indulgence, but without some kind of financial plan (budget) most couples won't realize they have a problem until it overwhelms them.

Many people think they live on a budget because they record the amount of the checks written, dutifully write down debit card uses, keep track of on-line bill payments, and even balance their checking accounts by regularly viewing activity online.

That is not a budget. A budget balances income and expenses and reports on the status of those each month. I'm not going to discuss the subject of budgeting here, because I have done so in several previous books, including a thorough plan outlined in *The Family Financial Workbook*. (Be sure to take advantage of the Resources section in the back of this book.) Instead, I am going to discuss some of the more common ways couples get into debt.

A HOME

Part of the American dream seems to be home ownership. I use the term "own" loosely, because what that means to most people is to be paying a mortgage. So the common definition of owning is "as opposed to renting." Many people try to buy a home too soon or pay too much, and end up in financial trouble.

Unfortunately, quite often they don't realize that financing the home created their monetary troubles because it took too large a portion of their spendable income. Just as with Ben and Naomi, the first couple discussed in this book, they find themselves sinking further behind every month.

The percentage of an average family's budget that should be spent on a house payment is no more than 32 to 40 percent of net spendable income (after tithes and taxes). That percentage would include mortgage payments, utilities, insurance, maintenance, and incidentals.

Unfortunately, many couples commit more than 60 percent of their budgets to housing. There is virtually no way to handle that kind of cost. If they look at their spending for the year, the strain would be apparent, but, because they usually look only at one month, they don't see it. The monthly budget an individual or family has typically lacks allocations for clothes, car repairs, and medical expenses. So it is unrealistic.

If you can afford to purchase a home within your budget, it's a good decision to buy. But wrecking your budget just to own a house makes no sense at all. The compulsion Americans have for buying large, expensive homes is just a reflection of poor stewardship in general. Most couples would be far better off saving for a down payment of at least 20 percent and buying a smaller, less expensive home initially. Certainly the purchase of a home for a young couple should never be determined on the basis of their combined incomes, because if one income fails (for example, if the wife becomes pregnant and stays home with the child) the entire purchase will be in jeopardy. That violates the principle of good planning: "A prudent man sees danger and takes refuge, but the simple keep going and suffer for it" (Proverbs 22:3).

Too often Christians limit their faith in God only to the unseen things, such as salvation; but I happen to believe that God manifests Himself in material ways to those who trust Him. And I do believe God wants to support strongly those who love and trust Him, just as a parent does a loving and obedient child. After all, that is what the Lord told us: "If you, then, though you are evil, know how to give good gifts to your children, how much more will your Father in heaven give good gifts to those who ask him!"(Matthew 7:11).

A CAR

The second most common source of debt is the purchase of a new car. Quite often a couple who can't qualify to buy a home springs for a new car as a compromise. Unfortunately, it's not a good compromise because cars now sell for prices that houses sold for a few decades ago. This is the major debt trap for most singles who overspend.

Most people are so prone to debt-buying today that they don't even ask the price of a car—just how much the monthly payments are. I believe the automotive industry understands this mentality very well. When they want to stimulate sales for a product that has been inflated out of proportion to most other consumer products, they advertise low interest rates as the biggest selling feature. Usually that is the deciding factor for a generation that has been raised on new cars and nice houses. To the young couple already in debt because of a home that is too expensive, a new car appears to be an answer to their used car problems. So they trade in the old car, which costs money every month to keep running, for a new car with a greater monthly payment (plus gas, oil, and upkeep). But it's not good economics, as they will discover in about two months (the first month is usually free).

A family seeking to sell an almost new car to relieve debt is usually shocked to discover how little it's worth on the open market. If it's sold at auction, which is often the case when a car is repossessed, the sale price may be half of what an identical car sells for on a lot. Typically, when a car is repossessed for failure to make the payments, the car is sold at a loss, and the lien holder sues the borrower for the difference.

The same is true of a leased car. The lease contract to pay is just as binding as a purchase agreement. If the leasing company has to repossess a leased car, it rarely will attempt to lease it again. The typical lessee wants a brand-new car, not a used one. The leased car is auctioned off, and the leaseholder is sued for the deficiency.

I have sometimes been accused of being negative about new cars, and to some extent that is true. Over the years I have seen the bondage that buying new cars has placed on many people. However, if someone has his or her finances under control and can save for the cost of a new car, it is his or her decision whether to buy one. One person may think a new car is a bad buy, but another may think it represents better value. The one thing neither of them can disagree about is that when you borrow money to buy a new car, you have purchased something that depreciates in value almost immediately.

For most of my adult life I never bought a new car, for two reasons: one, I didn't have the funds to pay for one, and, two, I couldn't see the need for one with so many good used cars available. At one point I was driving a ten-year-old station wagon with well over 100,000 miles on it, and I knew that I would have to buy another car within a short time. Then one of our sons attempted to back my car up our very steep driveway during a minor ice storm. Backing up our driveway in good weather was a real trick, but it was impossible in bad weather. Like most teenagers, he was not to be dissuaded by a "small" obstacle such as an ice storm, so he kept trying until he burned out the reverse gear.

The next time I got into my car, I discovered it whirred but wouldn't move in reverse. So we got several of the neighborhood kids out and pushed the car around in the driveway so that I could pull up the hill. For several weeks I drove it anyway, while we all prayed about what kind of a car we should buy. It didn't seem logical to spend the money to repair the old wagon when it had so many miles on it.

We didn't really have enough money to buy a new car, but with my teaching schedule and frequent trips to the airport, I knew that we needed a dependable vehicle. During the next few weeks I discovered how many times you pull into a parking space that you have to back out of.

While we were praying about what to do, someone actually gave a car to the ministry. But it had a lot of miles on it too, so I figured I might as well keep the one I had and give the donated car to a really needy family. One of my children suggested that I give away the car with no reverse, but I vetoed that idea.

I drove my "no-reverse" car for several more months because the Lord directed us to use the money we had saved for another purpose. Then, in December, someone I had counseled several years earlier dropped by to ask if we had any particular need for a car.

"Why do you ask?" I said.

"Because I am convinced that the Lord wants me to give you one," he replied as he handed me the keys to a new Oldsmobile, which I drove for the next six years.

THE UNSCHEDULED

Do you know how to schedule a financial disaster? It's simple: just fail to plan for predictable expenses that haven't come due yet. A common example of this is failing to plan for routine automobile maintenance. I don't know about your cars, but mine have a regular cycle of problems. About every 25,000 to 30,000 miles they need tires, brakes, belts, spark plugs, and so on. Once I recognize that, the smart thing to do is to anticipate those expenses and budget for them.

Failure to plan this way is a major reason many people end up in debt. When the expenses occur, they must be paid, so the only alternative available is often a credit card.

Why do reasonably intelligent people fail to anticipate known expenses? Because when they try to work them into their spending plans (budgets), they don't fit. So they simply ignore those expenses until a crisis arrives. To do otherwise would require adjustments in other areas of spending, such as housing, cars, and vacations. This is the head-in-the-sand syndrome.

It was common to see this problem when I counseled engaged couples about their first year's budget. When I asked if they had developed a budget, usually they responded, "Yes, we have, and everything worked out fine."

But when I reviewed their budget with them, it revealed that they had made no provision for clothes, visits to the doctor, car repairs, or vacations. They might be able to convince me that they had a car that didn't break down, and bodies that didn't get sick, or even teeth that don't get cavities, but I absolutely refused to believe they weren't going to Disney World the first year they were married. And most people need to replace their clothes eventually.

I recall a couple who thought they had figured out a way to beat the system. They had financial problems that resulted from all of the above symptoms. In other words, they had a home that was too expensive, two new cars, school loans, and a variety of consumer debt items from department stores. There was absolutely no way their income could ever stretch far enough to manage their expenses, so they charged nearly everything each month, except their utilities (the utility company wouldn't accept credit cards). They had been able to do that for nearly three years without being delinquent on a single bill.

Their method was to charge on one card until the limit was reached and then pay that card off with two or three others. Being a good credit customer, they had no trouble getting their credit limit raised on the first card so they could charge more, and on they went for the better part of three years. Ultimately, the whole house of credit came tumbling down, because it became too large to manage. When their credit binge ended, they owed nearly $25,000 in credit card debts. They were advised to file for bankruptcy, and they were considering doing so, until they received notice that two of the credit card issuers were considering filing fraud charges against them.

The potential consequences of that wake-up call forced them to face reality and make major changes to their financial management, as well as commit to repay the loans.

PART THREE:

INFORMATION *at* YOUR SERVICE

C H A P T E R

MORE ABOUT CREDIT:

ESTABLISHING, AVOIDING, IMPROVING

Since we're discussing the subject of debt in this book, we also need to discuss credit.

Credit and debt are not synonymous terms, although they are used interchangeably in our society. Credit can best be defined as *the establishment of a mutual trust relationship between a lender and a borrower.*

Debt, as defined previously, is a condition that exists when a loan commitment is not met or inadequate collateral is pledged to unconditionally satisfy a loan agreement. Borrowing is not the only way to get into debt. A court decree in a lawsuit, for instance, can result in debt. But for the purpose of this book, we'll limit our discussion to credit-related debt.

GETTING (ESTABLISHING) CREDIT

Many young people get into trouble with credit because they are desperate to establish credit and because it is easy for them to qualify for more credit than they can manage.

The very best way to establish credit, initially, is to borrow against an acceptable asset. For example, if you have saved $1,000 and want to borrow the same amount, almost any bank will lend you $1,000, using the savings as collateral. Usually the lender will charge from 1 to 2 percent more for the loan than the prevailing savings rate. So, in essence, it costs about 2 percent interest to establish a good credit history. For a one-year loan of $1,000, the net cost would be approximately $20.

Then, by using the bank as a credit reference, almost anyone can qualify for a major credit card, although the credit limit would normally be the minimum amount. I don't mean to imply that everyone should get a credit card, or that everyone will be able to manage one properly. But credit is relatively simple to establish if you have already acquired the discipline of saving.

Credit card living has become a way of life for many people in our culture. It has been my experience that if someone who has never had credit wishes to acquire a credit card and tries enough places, somebody will issue one. The difficulty is that once the first company issues a card and the person uses it wisely, other companies will soon follow suit, and he or she will be swamped with credit card offers. The temptation of too much credit is often overwhelming for a young person (or couple) and for many other people, and serious indebtedness can be the result.

I offer the following advice to anyone using credit cards for the first time or who has ever gotten into trouble through the misuse of credit cards. It is good advice, and it will save you many problems.

1. Never use a credit card to buy anything that is not in your budget for the month—which means, in turn, that you will need a budget. It is tempting to use a credit card when you are on vacation and run out of your allocated vacation funds, or when you need clothes but don't have the money to take advantage of the great sale in progress, or when you need tires for the car but don't have the money saved, or when you're out of work and need food, utilities, and rent.

2. Pay the entire credit card bill each month. I've heard many people say that they never misused their credit cards, because they paid them off each

month. But using credit cards—or any credit—wisely is not merely a matter of being able to pay them off on time. Credit cards are the number one tool for impulse buying in our society, and impulse buying is generally the prerequisite for indulgent buying. Simply put, consumers will buy things they don't need and pay more for them, using credit.

I often use a credit card when traveling, and I always pay it off each month. At one time I assumed that because I never paid any interest on credit card purchases, I was using my card wisely. I decided to challenge my own use of credit, so I stopped using the credit card for a month.

Almost immediately I began to notice that I was less prone to accept a motel's summary of the bill when I paid in cash. I also found that I had gotten lax about verifying restaurant bills because I had been using credit cards. I discovered once again that credit is less personal than cash in your pocket and that people tend to use it more carelessly.

If you don't pay the credit card charges every month, you will pay an excessive rate of interest. Paying high rates of interest represents poor stewardship. In addition, by accumulating credit card charges, you run the risk of debt.

3. The first month you find yourself unable to pay the total charges, destroy the cards. The problem is not the use of credit—it is the misuse of credit.

CREDIT REPORTS AND CREDIT SCORES

You are entitled to a free credit report from each of the three national consumer reporting agencies every twelve months.[1] A credit report will include information on where you live, how you pay your bills, and other information about your credit history.

The information on your credit report will affect whether or not you can get a loan, and what the interest rate will be. You'll also want to periodically check your report for accuracy. If you'd like to compare the information from all three agencies, you'll want to send for the reports at the same time. However, it may be advantageous to spread out these free reports over the course of a year.

Your FICO (Fair, Isaac & Co) score is a three-digit credit score compiled from the credit bureaus.[2] These scores range from 300–850, the higher the better. If your credit score is low, it may be due to late payments of bills, amounts owed, too many credit accounts, or lack of credit history. The reporting agency Equifax offers tips for improving scores, as does Consumer Credit Counseling Service.[3]

If there are problems with or inaccuracies in your credit report, you'll want to take steps to correct them.[4] You'll also want to find ways to improve your credit score. Crown Financial Ministries has resources to help.[5]

CREDIT TO AVOID

There are some sources of credit that are simply bad deals. In the constant drive to create more ways for people to borrow money, many lenders have stepped over the borderline of common sense, in my opinion. But it is the responsibility of the borrower to avoid the use of credit that encourages poor stewardship. Following are a few examples of credit sources to avoid.

Bank Overdrafts

Most banks today offer what is called overdraft protection. Thus, when a customer writes a check or uses a debit card in excess of what he or she has in the bank, the payment will be honored (paid by the bank).

Sounds like a good deal, doesn't it? After all, if you write a check or use your debit beyond your balance, you don't want to be overdrawn, do you? There would be penalties for the returned check and charges from the merchant as well. So why not take the overdraft protection?

I have counseled many couples who did take the overdraft protection and got deeply in debt as a result of it. The people who regularly go into overdraft are those who don't know their checking account balances. Obviously there are those who are dishonest and purposely overdraft, but they are a minority and usually can't get overdraft protection anyway.

Some banks automatically enroll customers who are setting up a new account in an overdraft protection plan. Banks generally charge twenty to thirty dollars per transaction.[6] Other overdraft protection plans involve linking a checking account to a savings account or to a credit card. If you write a check or use an ATM without sufficient funds, the bank will transfer funds from one account to another and charge you for it.[7]

The overdraft protection is an enticement for people to avoid balancing their checking accounts. Several people I have counseled were startled to find out that overdraft protection wasn't a benevolent act on the part of the bank. The overdrafts (and penalties) were charged to their credit accounts at 18 to 21 percent interest. Often those accounts accumulate interest from the date of transfer, not after the normal thirty days common to credit card accounts.

Finance Company Loans

I don't want to impugn the integrity of all finance companies, because there are many honest and ethical companies in business. But, in general, local finance companies, especially those not regulated by federal laws, use high-pressure tactics in their operation and charge very high interest. For instance, in many states, finance companies that limit their loans to $600 or less can charge interest rates that go as high as 40 percent per year!

Finance companies specialize in lending to those who can't qualify for loans through normal channels, such as banks, credit unions, or savings and loans. They also specialize in high-pressure tactics to collect their money if necessary. If you are being pursued by one of these companies, you need to know your rights under the Fair Debt Collection Act.[8]

Home Equity Loans

Some people might wonder why I place home equity loans in this section about credit to avoid. After all, home equity loans are one of the few loans still available where the interest may be able to be deducted from one's income taxes.

In general, these loans have several features that make them hazardous to an individual's long-term financial health. First, they encourage someone to borrow against the equity of the home when in truth he or she should be working to pay the remaining mortgage off.

Second, the interest rates are usually floating, meaning that they can be adjusted as the prevailing interest rates change. That puts the borrower in a position in which it is nearly impossible to control future costs.

Third, most of these loans (to date) are demand notes, meaning they can be called for total payment at any time. This places the debtor in the position of constant jeopardy with the lender. During a bad economy, the lender is likely to call the note to renegotiate the terms or sell the collateral (your home).

Payday Loans

Another source of credit to avoid is payday loans. Businesses that offer these loans are legal in thirty-nine states, though nearly a dozen ban such loans.

The problem with payday loans is that most borrowers can't afford repayment and need to borrow again to pay off their initial loans. The average rate on these loans runs about 400 percent annually.

The Center for Responsible Lending figured that a loan of $325 took $793 to repay. The center figured an average fee of $52 and "multiplied it by nine to account for the number of times such a loan is flipped into a new one." Thus, a customer is paying a fee of $468 in order to pay back the original loan of $325.[9]

Set Aside Tax Money

If there is one source of credit you should diligently avoid, it is the IRS — or to put it another way, don't live on money that you owe to the IRS. I have counseled many couples who attempted to do this, especially couples who were self-employed. They found that the IRS will attach every asset to collect their money and will force a sale at drastically reduced prices if necessary.

IMPROVING YOUR CREDIT

If you have or have had credit problems, you can take action to improve your credit rating. Nothing is a quick fix, but now is the time to begin.

Paying your bills on time is the first step in improving credit. If you have missed payments, work to get current and then stay current. Keep your balances on credit cards low, and pay off debt rather than moving it from card to card. If you open a new account and pay it off in a timely manner, you can raise your credit score.[10]

Again, checking your credit report will help you find items that should be cleaned up, such as items that are more than seven years old, accounts that are noted as anything besides "current" if you have paid them off, even charges that do not belong to you.[11] Correcting these matters will raise your credit score.

DETERMINING THE TRUE INTEREST RATE

In conclusion to this discussion on credit, it is vital that you understand how to determine the true interest rate someone is quoting to you. The Truth in Lending Act now requires that all interest be stated in Annualized Percentage Rate (APR). That establishes one standard for all interest charged, regardless of how it is calculated. Let me present an example. If you borrowed $100 for one year and at the end of twelve months repaid $110, you had an APR of 10 percent.

But suppose you borrowed $100 and made monthly payments of $9.17. At the end of one year you would have repaid $110, but the Annualized Percentage Rate would have been higher. Why? Because you didn't actually have use of the entire $100 for the whole year. The APR rate was closer to 12 percent.

Additionally, the Truth in Lending Act requires that all finance charges be shown clearly before you sign an installment contract. Many times service fees, discount points, and insurance fees can substantially increase the cost of a loan.

A lender who fails to reveal all the costs risks penalties and forfeiture of all accumulated interest. If you believe you have been the victim of unfair lending, you need to contact the attorney general's office of your state.

In the final analysis, the best protection you can have against the misuse of credit is to determine that you will control the use of credit and refuse to allow it to control you. As stated earlier, there is no substitute for personal discipline and self-control in the area of credit.

By now I trust that you understand that the misuse of credit—not credit itself—is the problem. The Bible does not teach that you can never borrow; it teaches that borrowing is hazardous if done unwisely. Every Christian should have a goal to be debt-free eventually. If you can't be debt-free right now, set a goal and work toward it.

CHAPTER 12

BILL CONSOLIDATION

Allen and Sherry came into my office, obviously stressed. They were nervous about being there and embarrassed to tell me their story. Allen was an attorney with a local firm that specialized in real estate syndications. Just four years out of law school, Allen appeared to be the epitome of success. He was rising fast in the law firm because of his quick mind and hard work. He and Sherry had just bought a home in an exclusive section of their city and were expecting their first child. Their situation looked good, when viewed from the outside.

Inside, however, it was a different matter. When Allen graduated from law school, he owed a substantial amount in school loans. The interest rate on the loans was lower than average, but the monthly payments still would be made for ten years. Sherry had school loans also, though she didn't owe as much as Allen, and her monthly payments were more manageable. The loan payments restricted their spending but were within Allen's income capacity.

Within the last two years, Allen's salary and bonus had increased nicely, and his future prospects looked bright. They felt they could afford a better home and had decided to take the plunge and buy in the area where other, older members of the firm lived. They lacked the funds for the total down payment, but Allen arranged an advance on his bonus to close on the house.

When they moved, Sherry purchased custom curtains, drapes, and wall decorations with Allen's encouragement. He said (and believed) that what they were doing was in the best interest of his career. Before they were finished decorating and paying for moving costs, their bills totaled nearly $25,000.

By that time Sherry was beginning to feel a little nervous about their spending, particularly since they didn't have the money to pay for all their expenses. Allen told her not to worry, because the sale of their first home would net enough to pay back the advance and the improvements to the new home. Indeed, they did have a contract on their first home that would net them a profit. Unfortunately, the contract had an "if" clause in it, which meant that the buyers were obligated only if their home sold. So Allen and Sherry bought a new home, along with all the trappings, based on the contingent sale of their old home, which was dependent upon the sale of the buyers' home (a lot of ifs). It's obvious that no one had ever explained to them the principle, "Do not boast about tomorrow, for you do not know what a day may bring forth" (Proverbs 27:1).

As you probably have guessed, the sale of the buyers' home fell through, so they backed out of the purchase of Allen and Sherry's home. Allen and Sherry were already making payments on the new home, and they were continuing payments on their old home as well. To say the least, Sherry was uneasy about their situation. Each month they fell further behind, and still their house didn't sell. She wanted to lower the asking price, but Allen didn't agree, stating that it was worth what they were asking.

Finally, after six months, they had an offer on the house, though it was for many thousands of dollars less than the original contract. By that time Allen was glad to sell; they faced a higher mountain of unpaid bills each month. Virtually all the profit they made on the house went toward delinquent bills and repaying the firm. In the meantime they had accumulated another few thousand dollars in debts from miscellaneous sources.

Allen finally realized that their monthly obligations were beyond his income. So he approached the bank that held his new mortgage and asked about consolidating all of their outstanding bills into one loan. By that point, he needed about $20,000 to consolidate everything. The banker was a client of Allen's firm and thought that he would be a good risk, but Allen lacked adequate collateral for a loan that size. After a great deal of negotiating, they found a way to make the loan by taking out a second mortgage on their home and assigning that year's bonus as additional collateral.

Since the monthly payments on a $20,000 loan for three years would have been beyond Allen's income range, the banker set the payments based on a ten-year payoff, but with a balloon note to be paid in seven years (the maximum time the bank would grant for a second mortgage). It was further agreed that at least $5,000 of each year's bonuses would be paid to the bank to reduce the note.

The first year everything went fine, or so it seemed. Allen earned a bonus of $15,000. He paid $5,000 on the note, put $5,000 in savings, and paid nearly $4,000 in taxes on the bonus. With the rest, he and Sherry took a vacation to a ski resort that winter.

Allen kept track of their accounts at home and repeatedly told Sherry not to worry about it, so Sherry didn't really have a clear idea of how they were doing month by month. But she began to see late notices coming from the bank and several credit card companies. Finally she asked Allen to sit down and tell her exactly where they were financially. He confessed that even he didn't really know. "It just seems like there is never enough money to pay everything we owe," he said. He agreed with Sherry that they needed to do something about their budget. But then he got busy on a new project, and they never got around to it.

As the late notices became more frequent, Sherry began to complain to Allen that he had to get some help in handling their situation. He agreed but never took the time to search for the help he needed. Finally, one afternoon the whole situation came to a head when his banker called Allen at his office. "Allen, I need to see you right away. Can you come by my office this afternoon?" he asked.

"Doubtful; this is a busy time," Allen replied as he looked over the contracts on his desk. He had been getting less and less productive as the pressures at home built. It seemed that Sherry was always irritated about one thing or another.

"Allen, I must see you right away," Gary Barnes insisted. "The loan committee has been reviewing your note with the bank and is recommending that we begin foreclosure on your home."

Allen felt a cold wave of fear come over him. "They can't do that," Allen pleaded. "It would ruin me with the firm. We have very strict rules about maintaining a good image in the community."

"Come on over, and let's discuss it, Allen. Maybe there is a way we can find a resolution."

Allen put down the phone, his hand shaking. He knew he had financial problems, but until that moment he hadn't realized how bad they were. He was three months behind on his first mortgage and four months behind on the second. He had been promising the bank that he would catch up on the payments when his midyear bonus came. But that bonus had been just $6,500, and it had been used to cover draws from the firm for living expenses. Allen's manager had called him in to review his work for the past six months because his productivity had dropped off severely. He knew that the bank's repossessing his home might cost him his job, and he was only a year away from being made a full partner in the firm. His salary and bonuses would increase substantially then. He felt cold fear rising inside as he realized that not only might he not get a partnership, he might even be released from the firm. He had survived one round of layoffs but didn't have any guarantees that he would survive another.

Allen put down his work and left the office, telling the receptionist he would be back in an hour or so. He entered the bank and asked if he could see Gary Barnes, who was the vice president of the loan department. In a short while he was directed to the banker's office.

"Allen, sit down, won't you?" the banker said politely. He walked over and closed the door to his office. "You have some severe financial problems, don't you?" he asked.

"Well, we do have some temporary problems, Gary," Allen replied. "But I'll be able to clear them up when the next bonus comes."

"You need to face reality," Gary said as he opened the file on his desk. "I took the liberty of checking into your recent credit history. You're behind on everything, even your utility payments."

"It seems that there's not enough money to make it every month," Allen explained. "But I'll be a partner in the firm in a few months, and my income will increase substantially then. Can't you extend the second mortgage? I would only need a few thousand dollars more to make it until then."

"No, I absolutely will not. It's not more money you need, and another consolidation loan won't help. You're simply digging yourself a bigger pit. You're living beyond your means and using loans to make up the difference. And you'll just continue to do so, no matter how much you make. I did you a disservice by giving you the first consolidation loan on your house. You're worse off now than you were then."

Allen slumped down in his chair. He wanted to argue with the banker, but he knew that he was telling the truth. They were worse off now, and there seemed to be no end to the flood of money going out. With a new baby, Sherry wasn't in a position to work, so it was all up to him.

"What can I do?" Allen asked in a subdued tone. "If you foreclose on my home, I may lose my job."

"Allen, I found that one of the credit card issuers is planning legal action to collect their money. You may well be facing a judgment and garnishment if they do."

Allen almost felt faint when he heard that news. *That definitely will cost me my job,* he thought. "What do you suggest?" he asked, numb.

"I want you to go to a financial coach who will help you to work out a plan. I know him well, and we'll work with you in whatever action he decides you should take."

Allen called the coach for a meeting, and he asked him to come in the next day with Sherry. The solution to Allen and Sherry's problems was difficult but not complicated.

The coach, Art Hill, said the first step was to get an accurate picture of where they stood financially, and asked them to withhold nothing. Together they listed every debt and found that Allen and Sherry had accumulated nearly $3,000 in additional debt since the consolidation loan. Basically they were back on the same track they had been on before the loan, but with greater expenses each month because of the second mortgage.

They were also delinquent on almost every debt, including a Master-Card bill that had not been paid in five months. Their basic household expenses, together with minimum payments on their debt, took 120 percent of their income, including the average bonus Allen received.

Even before Allen took on the consolidation loan, their average monthly expenses consumed over 95 percent of their income without such costs as clothes, medical, and dental bills. The consolidation loan allowed them to avoid the reality of a bad situation for a few more months. They were unable to give anything to their church, even though both Allen and Sherry had been tithing Christians since their youth. During the past several months, they had stopped going to church and rarely prayed together, even though that also had been their commitment since before they were married. As with most couples experiencing financial problems, they simply lacked the desire to seek the Lord together.

Allen contacted the bank that issued the MasterCard, and it agreed to accept a minimum payment on the account for three months while it worked with Art Hill to work out a permanent resolution. Art then contacted Gary Barnes at the bank and arranged for the bank to accept a three-month moratorium (no payments) on the second mortgage, provided that the first mortgage was brought up to date during the following month.

The plan was simple and direct. Both Allen and Sherry realized that they were in over their heads financially and that they had to reduce their expenses. There were only two areas that could be cut substantially: housing and autos. The house and one car had to be sold if they were ever to balance their budget. Both decisions were difficult for them to accept until all the figures were on the table and visible. Then the facts dictated the decisions. They could stay in their home until it was repossessed or sell it voluntarily. They could drive one new car or lose them both. These were tough facts but easy decisions.

They had only one asset that could be converted into immediate cash to pay the bank: a cash value insurance policy that Allen had owned for several years. It had nearly $3,000 in cash value, and they used it to bring the first mortgage to a current status.

They put the house up for sale, and when it finally sold, they recovered enough from the sale to pay off the credit cards and much of the second mortgage. The bank willingly agreed to carry a note for the remaining amount, which was paid off within the next year.

Allen and Sherry rented a nice apartment and worked hard to get their finances under control. They developed a realistic budget and began to give to their church each month. Eventually they used their own experiences to help with classes in their church, teaching on biblical principles of handling money.

Allen became a partner in the law firm and ten years later was made the senior partner in the real estate department. He instituted a policy that all new attorneys joining the firm must attend a class on budgeting and agree to live on a budget for the first year. His feeling was that if he could get them to live on a budget for a year, they would live on one forever. He tells his story to every new attorney and proudly points out that he and Sherry were able to purchase an affordable home, which they own debt-free.

IS A CONSOLIDATION LOAN ALWAYS WRONG?

One of the most common questions asked in coaching is, "Should we consolidate?" So the logical question a Christian needs to ask is, "Is it wrong to consolidate?"

The answer is no, not necessarily. But there are some inherent problems that must be dealt with before a consolidation loan is advisable.

First, unless the problems that created the need for a consolidation loan are corrected, you may find yourself worse off in the long run. For instance, if the debt was created by overspending on a monthly basis, the consolidation loan won't solve that problem. It will only delay the inevitable. Until the problem of overspending is solved, no consolidation loans should ever be considered. Otherwise, a year or so later all the little bills will be back again, and when they are combined with the consolidation loan, the situation will be worse.

I recommend that no one consider a consolidation loan until he or she has been living for six months on a budget that controls overspending. Once that person has the overspending under control, it may make sense to substitute one large loan at a reduced interest rate for several smaller ones at higher rates.

Second, with a consolidation loan, there is always the tendency to stop worrying once the supposed solution has been found. Many people actually spend more the month after consolidating than they ever did before, often taking vacations or buying new televisions or computers. Why? Because they think the pressure is off and they can relax. That is a false security created by the temporary removal of financial pressure. They should resist that urge to splurge.

Third, all too often when someone consolidates, he or she borrows more than what is needed to pay the outstanding bills. Then that person buys things he or she has wanted for several months but wasn't able to afford. The purchases may actually be needed items, such as a refrigerator, a washing machine, or a car.

What's wrong with that? Nothing, as long as the individual is disciplined enough to save the money to buy those things. But for those who already have discipline problems, it's just one more way to splurge.

In our culture there are almost limitless temptations to spend. Thousands of people actually make their living by thinking of new ways to lend money and collect interest. Perhaps the most common method of consolidating has become the home equity loan. Since the 1986 Tax Reform Act[1] made home loans virtually the only interest deductible on income taxes, more and more people have turned to home equity loans for consolidating.

I personally believe home equity loans are one of the worst ideas ever pushed on the average family. It encourages them to put their homes in jeopardy and borrow to buy things that they can easily do without, such as new cars.

SOURCES OF CONSOLIDATION LOANS

There are several places where people can obtain a consolidation loan.

Cash Value Insurance

An often-overlooked source of funds for consolidating is the cash value in an insurance policy. That money can normally be borrowed at far less than market rates. Even if you don't have a cash value policy, perhaps a parent does and would be willing to lend it to you.

Pledged Collateral

Most banks will provide loans at 1 or 2 percent below the market rate, and in-bank deposits are used as collateral. Obviously, not many people who need consolidation loans have spare cash that can be used as collateral, but often family members do. This requires a high degree of trust on the part of the family member, because the collateral is at risk if the loan is not repaid. I do not recommend this option unless the borrowers are in a financial coaching program in which someone is monitoring their finances at least monthly.

A collateralized loan is certainly better than a cosigned note, which is highly discouraged in Scripture. With pledged collateral, someone might lose the asset, but with a cosign, that person can potentially lose what he or she doesn't have.

Credit Unions

Many people have access to credit union loans at lower-than-market rates. As long as all the previously mentioned cautions are observed, a credit union loan is one of the better sources of consolidation.

Family Loans

Unless the family member (usually a parent) is able and willing to lose the money, I discourage this option, particularly when the parent is not a Christian and the child is. I have seen many parents discouraged and hurt because their children failed to meet their financial obligations. I believe Satan uses this as a stumbling block to a parent's salvation. Obviously if the parent is a Christian and is willing to absorb the loss (if necessary), there is nothing wrong with parental loans.

However, a word of caution to parents is in order here. If you continually bail your children out of their financial difficulties, you are doing them a great disservice. If you want to help, be sure you require your children to get the counsel they need first. Remember, more money is not the answer to most financial problems. More discipline is the answer.

Retirement Accounts

Normally money saved in a retirement account, such as an IRA, should be left there for that purpose. However, if no other source of funds is available, you can invade the retirement account and withdraw funds. Be aware that there will be income taxes due and a 10 percent penalty.

Borrowing from an employer-sponsored retirement plan, such as a 401(k), is possible under certain circumstances, but strict rules govern this action. Check with your company benefits department for information and guidelines.

DEALING *with* CREDITORS

The way someone deals with creditors says a lot about that person's character and spiritual maturity. The Lord said, "Settle matters quickly with your adversary who is taking you to court. Do it while you are still with him on the way, or he may hand you over to the judge, and the judge may hand you over to the officer, and you may be thrown into prison" (Matthew 5:25). That's merely a confirmation of the principle, "The rich rule over the poor, and the borrower is servant to the lender" (Proverbs 22:7).

Many times I have seen Christians take up an offense against a creditor who is especially aggressive about wanting payment of a debt. But although we have legally limited a lender's ability to collect the money owed, that does not negate the lender's authority over the borrower.

The principle to remember is, to always run toward your creditors, not away from them. A very difficult problem to overcome is attempting to negotiate with a creditor who has been ignored for a long time. Put yourself in the position of a creditor. Wouldn't you want to know that someone was willing to pay but couldn't, rather than to be left totally in the dark?

Unfortunately, many people who can't pay everything don't pay anything. That is also an error. Pay what you can each month, even if it's only a partial payment. And don't make unrealistic promises in order to get a creditor off your back. You need to approach a promise to pay with the same degree of caution that you would the signing of a contract. When you give your word, you need to keep it. If you make a promise when you know that you won't be able to meet the terms, you have violated the principle of vows. Listen to what the judge said about vows: "When you make a vow to God, do not delay in fulfilling it. He has no pleasure in fools; fulfill your vow. It is better not to vow than to make a vow and not fulfill it" (Ecclesiastes 5:4–5).

HAVE A WRITTEN PLAN

I have found consistently that creditors respond best to a specific request that is backed by a detailed plan in writing.

Most creditors have been deceived so many times by people making desperate promises that they have become calloused. Almost anyone under the threat of a court summons or wage attachment will make the appropriate promises. Consequently, most creditors have developed immunity to tearful pleas from delinquent debtors. However, most will respond to a written plan backed by guaranteed action on the part of a debtor.

That's why a financial coach is often necessary in dealing with belligerent creditors. A coach generally represents an objective third party who will enforce the agreements.

Step 1: A Detailed Report

You need to state in detail exactly how much you owe and what the minimum monthly requirements are. You can find helpful forms online.[1] The chart below reproduces one of those forms.

It's vital to be totally honest and as accurate as possible. That's why I always work with both the husband and the wife in developing a debtors' list. One partner will often overlook something that the other will recall. The obvious difficulty is that if one spouse is hiding something from the other, he or she will avoid recording it in the creditor listing.

LIST OF DEBTS

as of _____

To Whom Owed	Contact Name / Phone Number	Pay Off	Payments Left	Monthly Payments	Date Due	Interest Rate

Since financial problems are usually accompanied by other problems, it is not unusual for one spouse to try to continue the deception if he or she is afraid of the reaction the truth will evoke. If you are in debt, I encourage you to be honest with your spouse. There is no way one person alone can resolve a debt problem that affects two people.

If you're the offended party, try to control your reaction to any new revelation about your finances. Your response will often determine whether your spouse will be honest in the future.

If you are the offending party, you need to accept the risks involved with total honesty and lay all the finances out on the table (literally). Ultimately the truth will be revealed anyway, and the reaction will be worse, the longer it is delayed. Lying and deception are sins, and God has said there will be consequence for sin. He also promised that if we confess our sin, He is faithful to forgive us and cleanse us (see 1 John 1:9).

Step 2: A Budget

Once the creditor list is complete and accurate, the next step is to develop a budget that will tell you and the creditors how much you can pay them each month.

In the chart I have depicted a typical budget from couples who come to Crown Financial Ministries for budget coaching. The left side shows their budget based on their previous spending records.

The amounts on the right represent the new budget submitted to the creditors. Notice that the amount allocated for debts doesn't match the previous monthly total calculated from the creditor's chart. The only thing that can be done is to ask the creditors to accept a lesser amount for a period of time. Before that request can be made, however, we need to know how long that period will be. Often that depends on whether or not there are assets that can be sold and how long it will take to sell them. Also the option of a consolidation loan must be considered if it will satisfy all the creditors.

Obviously, creditors are not going to agree to a plan that provides them with no payments if there is no promise of an appreciable change in the future. But I have often seen creditors accept smaller payments for a period of time when there does appear to be a logical reason for the temporary reduction. If the reduced payments are within 75 percent of the actual payments,

GROSS PER YEAR: $60,000
GROSS PER MONTH: $5,000
NET SPENDABLE INCOME PER MONTH: $3,600

MONTHLY BUDGET	EXISTING	NEW
1. Tithe	$ 500	$ 500
2. Taxes	$ 900	$ 900
NET SPENDABLE INCOME (per month)	$3,600	$3,600
3. Housing	$ 1,630	$ 1,580[a]
4. Food	$ 500	$ 500
5. Automobile(s)	$ 775	$ 525[b]
6. Insurance	$ 200	$ 170[c]
7. Debts	$ 300	$ 175[d]
8. Entertainment/Recreation	$ 350	$ 150[e]
9. Clothing	$ 75	$ 75
10. Savings	$ 0	$ 85[f]
11. Medical	$ 100	$ 100
12. Miscellaneous	$ 240	$ 240
13. School/Child Care	$ 0	$ 0
14. Investments	$ 300	$ 0[g]
TOTALS (Items 3 through 14)	$4,470	$3,600
	($870)	(balanced)

[a] Reduced cable TV package, sanitation, and Internet package

[b] Sold second car which eliminated 1 car payment

[c] Dropped whole life insurance policy – bought cheaper 20-year term policy.

[d] Paid off two loans with car proceeds

[e] Reduced entertainment by not going out to eat as much

[f] Increased the emergency fund

[g] Discontinued investing until adequate savings were established and more debts were paid off

there is usually no difficulty in getting the creditors to accept a reduced payment plan indefinitely. Obviously that depends on the creditor. Some are restricted by company policies. In those cases it is often necessary to appeal to higher management. In almost all cases they will require a third party to negotiate on behalf of the debtor.

Many companies have a working agreement with the national Consumers Credit Counseling Service (CCCS), which is a nonprofit group of credit counseling agencies located in most major cities. They can usually negotiate reduced payment schedules as well as reduced interest fees.

Crown Financial Ministries has volunteer budget coaches located nationwide who assist individuals, free of charge, in establishing budgets that will help them become debt free and honor God through their finances.

What Happens When a Creditor Won't Cooperate?

Most attempts to get out of debt sound great because you usually hear the success stories. But what happens when the creditors refuse to cooperate? The principle to remember is this: don't give up too soon. Often when the debts are delinquent, the original lender has already turned the account over to a collection agency. The collection agency is less prone to cooperate and more likely to sue. But unless the debt has actually been sold to a third party, the original lender can still control the proceedings.

Generally speaking, the local credit office of a national company has only limited ability to negotiate once a loan has been declared delinquent. So your best chance to reach an agreement is to request the name of the regional or district credit manager and try to work out a settlement. You must suggest a reasonable plan.

However, there are times when the best efforts don't work. That is usually because the debtor has made frequent promises that were not kept or because he or she failed to respond to the many warnings the company sent out before pursuing legal action. The actions a creditor normally takes will fall into one of three areas.

Repossession

If you have borrowed for a specific asset such as a car, television, refrigerator, or furniture, and the asset is security for the loan, a creditor has the right to repossess it according to the terms of your loan agreement.

With rare exception those agreements give the creditor the right to repossess without written notice if the account is delinquent. (Many states do require written notice.) Most people have heard stories of professional car repossessors who sneak into the debtor's yard and pirate away the car. Indeed that does happen, and if a repossess order has been rendered, it is legal in most states.

More common is for a delinquent debtor to receive written notice that a creditor is taking action in court. Normally there is a legal waiting period (usually one month) during which you have the right to present your side, if there is a dispute. However, if a debtor ignores the notification and does not appear in court, the judgment award is automatic, and the creditor can and will repossess the assets.

I have received many an urgent phone call from a frantic homeowner whose house was about to be taken by foreclosure. Often I find out the day before the foreclosure hearing. It's usually too late then, unless the entire delinquent amount can be offered the lender. If a judgment has already been handed down, it may require the entire mortgage balance. Unfortunately, the lenders usually would have worked out a reasonable plan to avoid having to repossess the home, because of the expenses involved and the bad publicity that often accompanies such action. But once the legal process is started, it is difficult to abort.

Armed with a court order, a creditor can indeed come into a debtor's home to repossess an asset. If the collector is refused entry, on the next trip the repossessor can simply bring a sheriff's deputy, who will order the debtor to comply. Failure to comply with the court order can result in arrest and additional expenses.

Most loan contracts contain clauses that allow the creditor to collect all costs associated with legal action or repossessions. You need to read any contracts you sign very carefully because the costs of such actions can be significant.

Once the merchandise is recovered, the creditor may choose to sell it and apply the proceeds against the outstanding debt. The difference between the loan balance and the sale proceeds is called a deficiency, and the creditor has the right to bill the debtor for that amount plus all costs associated with the repossession and sale.

Garnishment

In states that allow it, a creditor can petition the court to attach the wages of a debtor once a legal judgment has been issued. This can be a great shock to the unsuspecting debtor, as well as a source of great embarrassment. Unfortunately, it usually occurs at a time when everything else is going downhill financially. I remember the first time I encountered a garnishment.

A pastor asked me to meet with a young couple who were having severe financial difficulties. They had misused credit cards, department store loans, retail appliance loans, and so on. They were unable to meet all their obligations, and rather than face the creditors, they had taken the traditional ostrich approach. One of the creditors was a leasing company that specialized in rent-to-own contracts for furniture and appliances. Once their account was sixty days past due, the leasing company moved swiftly and received a judgment to repossess the furniture. They then resold the furniture for a ridiculously low price to the same company that had sold it originally and then sued the young couple for the deficiency, plus $400 in collection fees.

The couple was sent notices that the company was filing suit but chose to ignore the warnings and did not go to court. Consequently, the company got a garnishment order and attached both of their salaries. It was a shock when the young wife's boss called her into his office and showed her the garnishment. The garnishment required that the employer withhold up to 25 percent of her wages to pay the judgment. For a family already having severe financial difficulties, that was a major crisis. The husband found that his wages were similarly attached.

Usually there is nothing that can be done once the judgment is finalized, but I remember this particular case because it had a somewhat happy ending. After some checking around, I found that the leasing company had had several complaints filed against it for reselling repossessed furniture to the original sales outlet at prices substantially below fair market value. I also learned that the retail store had several outstanding lawsuits against it for reselling used furniture as new.

Through a local attorney, we petitioned the court and got a rehearing. The judge withdrew the judgment and directed the leasing company to get three appraisals on the furniture in question as well as verification that the furniture had not been previously owned by another lease holder. The leasing company chose not to pursue the issue and dropped all collection proceedings against the couple. Thus the couple avoided the garnishment but needed the next four years to work out their other financial problems.

Bad Credit Report

In states in which a creditor cannot garnish a debtor's wages and the debt is noncollateralized (such as a credit card loan), the creditor has one last recourse: a bad credit report. Of course creditors will pursue collection through notices and telephone calls. But in the final analysis they must rely on the integrity of the borrower.

The purpose of a credit report is to notify other potential lenders that someone has failed to meet the conditions of a previous contract. The system relies on the fact that in our society people will need additional credit and thus will want to protect their credit rating. For a Christian the responsibility goes even further because the requirement to repay a debt is one of personal honor and integrity.

The reporting of your credit history is controlled by the Fair Credit Reporting Act. Basically this act governs the way a credit report is handled and gives the debtor certain rights.

1. The debtor has the right to know the name and address of the agency that prepared the report that was used to deny credit. To obtain that information, it is necessary to make the request in writing to any creditor that has refused credit.

2. Anyone refused credit has the right to review his or her file with the reporting agency. That person also has the right to obtain a copy of the case history file. The request must be made within thirty days of notification of credit refusal.

3. Someone who is refused credit has the right to challenge the information in the credit report if that information is inaccurate. If the dispute cannot be resolved, a letter containing the debtor's version of the dispute must be placed in the file and sent to prospective lenders.

4. Negative information cannot be reported beyond seven years, with the exception of a bankruptcy, which can be reported for up to ten years.

Because the Fair Credit Reporting Act forms the foundation for all cooperative credit reporting in this country, there are several other aspects of the Act with which all consumers should be familiar.

I have dealt with most of the major creditors in our country at one time or the other on the behalf of couples I have counseled, and as a member of the Consumer Counseling Service Board I have found that most creditors are willing to go to great lengths to help anyone in financial trouble who is trying to be honest and repay what is owed. But when a debtor lies and defaults on commitments that were made, he or she is likely to be faced with powerful and hostile adversaries. It is always best to be totally honest and not to make promises that cannot be kept just for the sake of temporary peace.

I also have found that few things make a better impression on a creditor than a well-thought-out budget plan, a list of all other creditors, and a credit card cut into several pieces as a testimony of commitment.

CHAPTER 14

LIVING *with* BANKRUPTCY

In 1980, there were just under 300,000 personal bankruptcies in our country. In 1990, there were more than 700,000, and in 2000, there were more than 1.2 million, according to the American Bankruptcy Institute. A tougher bankruptcy law, enacted in 2005, brought personal bankruptcy filings down to less than 600,000 the following year, but by 2008, personal bankruptcies had again crossed the 1 million mark.

A growing number of personal bankruptcies spells great difficulty for many smaller merchants and for the credit industry as a whole. But even more important, it reflects a decline in the responsibility index for the average American family, both Christian and non-Christian alike. Bankruptcies aren't limited to non-Christians. In fact, the percentage of Christians in bankruptcy appears to be about the same as that of the population in general, although accurate statistics are not readily available. I do know that an informal survey in almost any local church reveals a percentage approximating the national average.

The Bankruptcy Abuse Prevention and Consumer Protection Act of

2005 allows for several different types of bankruptcy.

Anyone considering bankruptcy action would be well advised to read up on bankruptcy[1] and then contact an attorney who specializes in this area.

Chapter 11 bankruptcy. This section of the bankruptcy code details how a corporation may file for federal bankruptcy protection and continue to operate while it works out a plan to repay the creditors. Under Chapter 11, some debts may be repaid and others may be discharged. The company may end contracts and leases and recover assets in order to increase its profitability.

This option was designed to give struggling companies that might otherwise fail a chance to become profitable and thus viable. For a great testimony on use of this bankruptcy law, I recommend the book *Parting the Waters* (Moody, 1997), which deals with the history of the Correct Craft company in Florida and its owners, Walt and Ralph Meloon.

Chapter 7 bankruptcy. A company seeking Chapter 7 bankruptcy protection must first undergo a means test to determine its ability to repay its creditors. If the company is found eligible for Chapter 7, its nonexempt assets are liquidated, and the proceeds are used to repay creditors. However, in some cases, all the company's assets may be determined to be secured.

Chapter 13 bankruptcy. This action is for individuals what the Chapter 11 bankruptcy is for a corporation. It allows an individual (or a couple) to repay certain debts under a court-approved plan during a period of up to five years. Other debts may be discharged.

Chapter 12 bankruptcy. This is a special provision for farmers and fishermen. It allows them to continue operating while repaying credits under a court-approved plan.

Is bankruptcy unscriptural? That is not a simple question to answer. God's Word clearly says that believers should be responsible for their promises and repay what they owe. Does that mean that in the meantime they should not take the legal remedy of court protection until they have the ability to repay? Often that is an individual decision. First and foremost, Christians must be willing to accept the absolute requirement to repay what they owe.

The issue of motive must be addressed. Is the action being taken to protect the legitimate rights of the creditors? I believe that answer can be found in asking whether assets are purposely withheld from the creditors. For example, many times when someone files for corporate or personal bankruptcy protection, assets have been transferred to the spouse or to other family members, as in the case of Bud's partners. If a husband and wife are treated as one, according to God's Word, then their assets must also be treated as one.

In general, the bankruptcy laws are meant to protect the debtor, not the creditor. But if the intent is merely to protect the assets of the debtor, it is unscriptural. It is better to suffer the loss of all assets rather than to lose one's integrity.

Here are some questions individuals and couples have asked about bankruptcy:

What effect will the Chapter 13 bankruptcy have on our future credit?

A credit reporting agency can report that you filed for bankruptcy protection for up to seven years after the date of that action. Chapter 7 bankruptcies can be reported for up to ten years. Therefore, any potential lender that inquires about your credit history will receive that report.

Is there any way to clear our credit rating?

Not really. Too often in our society people act as if there are no consequences of a bankruptcy, but that simply is not true. As already noted, a bankruptcy will appear on your credit report for seven to ten years. Even after this period, you may have some difficulty getting credit.

Is there any way we can prove that we are honest and reestablish a good credit rating?

Yes. Once the bankruptcy is cleared, you can continue to pay the entirety of the debts you owe. After a creditor is completely paid off, ask the creditor to write you a letter of recommendation and send a copy to the local credit reporting agencies. Many agencies will include letters of recommendation in their official credit reports. But you can also give the letters to a potential lender when you apply for a loan yourself.

The best recommendation I can give to anyone is to pay back what you borrow and never borrow frivolously. Remember, "A good name is more desirable than great riches; to be esteemed is better than silver or gold" (Proverbs 22:1).

What would happen if I lose my job for any reason?

If you're repaying debts under Chapter 13, notify your bankruptcy court trustee immediately to see about an adjustment to your plan.

Anyone who is not under a court order, such as a bankruptcy, needs to stay in direct contact with the creditors and tell them the absolute truth. Most creditors will work with a debtor who has temporary financial problems, as long as the debtor is trying to be fair and honest.

What about personal or corporate lawsuits?

In the present generation, it is not impossible or unlikely to be sued for millions of dollars over an accident. Also, considering the present climate in jury decisions, it is not uncommon to be assessed huge damage awards. Is it scripturally acceptable then to file for bankruptcy protection, rather than be wiped out financially because of an accident lawsuit? Again, there are no easy answers to that question. A Christian who is faced with such a dilemma needs to pray about the situation when it happens and trust in God's personal guidance.

I personally have no difficulty with those who use the court to avoid an unreasonable judgment. But because I want to protect myself from the costs incurred by another person's injury at my expense, I also choose to carry a sizable liability insurance policy that covers any accident in which I may be at fault. Beyond that amount I would feel the damages are punitive, rather than compensatory.

Can I avoid the IRS through a bankruptcy?

Many people are under the mistaken impression that going bankrupt avoids an obligation to the IRS. Let me assure you that this is not true. Under Chapter 13, you still must repay tax debt. Even under Chapter 7, many people still have to repay the IRS. In some cases, tax debt can be eliminated under Chapter 7, but only under limited circumstances. First of all, you must not be guilty of tax evasion. That may be easy if you're an honest person, but in addition, your debt to the IRS must involve income tax. Also, you must have filed a return for the taxes, which must be at least three years overdue. And, your tax debt needs to be declared at least 240 days before you file for bankruptcy.

I have worked with many people who have gone through bankruptcy. Some chose it voluntarily, and others had it forced on them by creditor actions. In both cases they quickly realized that bankruptcy is a serious matter, and at best both sides lose. The creditors lose much of the money they are owed, and the debtors lose some of the respect they previously had. There is a stigma associated with any bankruptcy, and until the last of the creditors are repaid, it will probably remain. You can turn an otherwise negative situation into a positive one by making a commitment to repay what is legitimately owed. You can only do what you can do. Once you have made the commitment, it is then up to God to provide the means.

Perhaps the scriptural principle that best describes the use of bankruptcy to avoid paying back legitimate debts is found in the parable of the unrighteous steward in Luke 16:1–12. In that parable the Lord describes a steward (a manager of another's property) who was guilty of misappropriating his master's property. When the master discovered what he had done, he determined to dismiss his steward. In an effort to maintain some security for himself, the manager negotiated with his master's clients and reduced the amounts they owed—apparently in hopes that they would pay him something later. When the master discovered that, he marveled at the ingenuity of the deceitful manager (verse 8).

Does the Lord also marvel at those who file for bankruptcy to avoid paying their creditors while holding assets that could be sold? Each Christian has to decide that issue individually. But what a shame it would be to appear before the Lord one day and learn, as Esau did, that an inheritance had been traded for a meal.

Remember, "No servant can serve two masters. Either he will hate the one and love the other, or he will be devoted to the one and despise the other. You cannot serve both God and Money" (Luke 16:13).

CHAPTER

WHERE *to* FIND HELP

T*he amount of my debt is fairly low, but I'd still like to pay it off and not accumulate more.*

The type of help a person in debt needs usually depends on the severity of the problems he or she is facing. If the problem is the overuse of credit cards and the total debt is a few hundred dollars, usually the solution can be worked out by writing up a good plan, as I described previously. In that case what is needed is a commitment to avoid further debt and a budget to verify that commitment.

Do I need an adviser before I consolidate my debts?

If a consolidation loan is needed to help bring the monthly payments in line with the income, the help of a good volunteer coach is beneficial. The danger of going deeper into debt is increased by the additional loan unless some monitoring takes place. That's the primary role of the volunteer coach: to be an objective observer and provide accountability.

We just don't see our way out of this mess.

As the problems intensify, the need for professional help arises. If the monthly payments exceed the available income and a reduced payment plan is required, then a coach who will intercede is almost always a necessity. Often a well-trained volunteer coach can help negotiate lesser payments or a moratorium on some payments until assets can be sold. But if a negotiated settlement cannot be reached, then additional help is required. This may be a professional credit counselor, an accountant, or an attorney.

Our situation has become critical and we need to go to court.

Once the problems have reached the legal action stage, the need for outside counsel becomes highly advisable. It is critical for a debtor to understand the rules of small claims courts or perhaps the bankruptcy court. That does not mean a debtor cannot handle any of those areas without professional help. With proper knowledge anyone can. I've seen many people plead their own cases in small claims court actions and several who were able to respond to a legal judgment notice properly. But they are the exceptions.

Proverbs teaches us that a wise person seeks the counsel of others. "Plans fail for lack of counsel, but with many advisers they succeed" (Proverbs 15:22). But another proverb tells us to weigh all counsel carefully. "A simple man believes anything, but a prudent man gives thought to his steps" (Proverbs 14:15).

What about the Bible?

One point must be made clear: God will not give us a direction in opposition to what He has already given in His Word. Thus the fundamental step is for an individual to understand what the Word of God says. Once he or she knows the rules for managing God's money, life becomes much easier for both the coach and the one being coached. If someone is not willing to follow the instructions given in God's manual, the best coach in the world can't help. A coach may deal with the immediate symptoms, but they will pop up again in a different place if the root problem is not resolved.

After this chapter, you'll see a list of Scriptures dealing with the subject of credit. The minimum that Christians should do is to spend a few minutes a day looking at those Scriptures and studying them. If they do that a couple of times, they will begin to get the flavor of what God's Word has to say about credit. As I have said consistently, credit is not prohibited, but it must be used properly.

Is it necessary that we seek counsel from a Christian source?

Of great importance to a Christian is the admonition to avoid the direct counsel of the unsaved. That in no way implies that unsaved people can't give good financial counsel. However, their counsel is lacking the most essential element: God's Word. It has been my experience that most counsel from unsaved financial advisers is aimed at protecting the assets of their clients, and that is to be expected. But Christians must focus on the rights of the other parties involved before their own. To do otherwise limits the ability of God to intercede on our behalf. The Bible says, "Trust in the Lord with all your heart and lean not on your own understanding; in all your ways acknowledge him, and he will make your paths straight" (Proverbs 3:5–6).

I believe the primary source of any counsel should be the local church. It's unfortunate that many churches aren't equipped to provide financial coaching for their people, though more are getting trained to do so every year. Usually there are Christian accountants, bankers, and businesspeople within the church who have the ability to help individuals with basic budgeting problems. If you need help, tell your pastor and ask him to refer you to someone in the church who can help on a volunteer basis. In general I have found that most people are willing to help and are even flattered by such a request. Most important, your request may stimulate the church to begin providing this needed ministry on a regular basis.

Our church wants to begin a financial ministry. Where do we start?

Churches interested in starting a financial ministry can become a part of a volunteer network established by Crown Financial Ministries. Go to crown.org for more information.

So what can I expect from a financial coach?

Too often those who ask for help from a financial coach expect too much too soon. Consequently, they become disillusioned when the coach doesn't have a magical formula that will make them debt-free in three months. Or, they expect the coach to tap the church treasury to bail them out of their troubles. In reality, fewer than 15 percent of the coaching cases I have seen (where the church was willing and able to assist them financially) actually needed direct financial support. With most of those, the financial help was temporary and only met basic needs.

A good coach will take an objective look at the total financial picture and then make recommendations that will resolve the problems permanently.

In most cases the answer for those in financial difficulties is personal discipline—not more money. Obviously there are exceptions, such as families in which a major illness has occurred or elderly people who are living on fixed incomes that are lower than the poverty level. Those are needs that must be met by other believers and generally are not one-time needs.

If there are urgent needs, such as pending foreclosures, judgments, or evictions, we try to deal with those immediately. But I make clear to everyone I counsel that there are no guarantees. If a foreclosure or eviction is imminent, it may be that nothing can be done to forestall it. Usually an experienced coach will have contacts to assist in finding temporary housing or transportation, but beyond that, his or her function is coaching—not funding.

From a coach's perspective, I can't emphasize strongly enough how many Christians expect unrealistic results from their advisers. Unfortunately, too many coaches foster those expectations by presenting themselves as authorities on a great variety of topics, ranging from sex to finances. Those assurances do help develop strong ties to the coach, but they are also self-defeating when those being coached discover the hard truth that there is no substitute for personal discipline.

I have been doing financial coaching for more than twenty-five years, and sometimes I think I have seen every possible problem and solution. Then someone comes up with an idea no one else has tried. Often when I pray with someone at the beginning of a coaching session, I am not really praying for them—I am praying for myself. I realize that I don't know all the answers, but I know that God does. If I can remember to draw from His wisdom, the persons coming to me for advice are not affected by my good or bad days.

I have coached several people whom I practically adopted. They became so dependent on my input that they literally refused to make a decision without talking to me first. Most coaches have experienced that at one time or another. At first I was flattered and allowed myself to be put in the position of becoming almost a substitute for the Holy Spirit in their lives (although that certainly was not my intent).

Then I discovered that they had become so paralyzed by their own mistakes that they no longer trusted their own judgment. Sometimes that is a predictable but temporary condition. For instance, someone who has suffered a trauma, such as a divorce or death of a spouse, may well need the support of an adviser. But beyond a few weeks (at the very most), that can become a crippling dependency. We all need others to counsel with and confide in, but God must be our permanent source of support.

I say this because I'm sure that some who read this book are depending too much on a particular adviser. A coach is there to guide you and offer alternatives but not to become a stand-in father or mother. Seek the face of God and His wisdom as your primary source of counsel, and you'll never be disappointed. If you find that one of your coaches is giving you advice contrary to God's Word, seek another coach.

I volunteer as a financial coach. Can you review the basics?

The basic coaching steps are as follows.

1. Determine the actual spending level at present. Rarely does a couple or a single person in debt know exactly how much it costs them to live each month. If they did, most already would have taken remedial action themselves. There are a variety of methods to determine how much they're presently spending. I personally begin by asking them by category how much they believe they spend each month.

Usually they have an estimated amount of spending, but rarely is it within 15 percent of the actual amount. I will add a fixed percentage for many incidental expenses such as clothing, car repairs, and vacations. Also, I know from experience that if they have never lived by a budget, their miscellaneous spending may be as much as 50 percent higher than they estimate.

2. Have those you are coaching keep a record of every expenditure they have for the next month. In rare cases the people have been writing checks or recording uses of their debit cards for every purchase, and their spending record can be determined from their checking account records, but only rarely. As you would expect, most persons in debt resist writing down every single purchase. I try to emphasize that this procedure is only necessary for one month—not for the rest of their lives. But it does require carrying a pocket notebook (and if it's a married couple, each must do this) for a month and writing down every penny they spend.

Once there is a clear picture of the actual monthly spending, the next step is to develop a budget that will provide for all of the regular household expenses to be paid, ideally with some money left over to pay the creditors. As was discussed previously, this may require some adjustments in the living expenses, especially in the areas of housing and auto.

3. Have those you are coaching maintain the budget each month. There are no quick fixes for most people who experience financial problems. As our examination of the finances of several couples showed, each had different circumstances and required unique solutions. But one common denominator was the need for accurate records and control over their spending.

In solving financial problems, accountability is a key ingredient that cannot be overemphasized. The value of consistent accountability has been proven through Alcoholics Anonymous, Weight Watchers, Celebrate Recovery, and small group Bible studies. The knowledge that someone will be checking to see if the checking account is balanced and the creditors paid helps to establish discipline.

Developing a support group in the community where you live can be a great asset to others who need help and accountability as well. I know of many groups that meet as often as once a week to discuss their common problems and try to come up with practical solutions. They also study what God's Word has to say about the subject of finances and hold each other accountable to apply those principles.

CREDIT-RELATED SCRIPTURES

SUBJECT:	SCRIPTURE:	COMMENTS:
BORROWING	Exodus 22:14	*Restitution for borrowed property*
	Exodus 22:15	*No restitution for rented property*
	Deuteronomy 28:43–45	*Disobey God and become borrower*
	Nehemiah 5:2–5	*Jews borrowing from Jews*
	Psalm 37:21	*Wicked does not repay*
	Proverbs 22:7	*Borrower is lender's slave*
	Isaiah 24:2	*Borrower will be like lender*
LENDING	Exodus 22:25	*Lend to brothers without interest*
	Deuteronomy 15:6	*Lend but not borrow*
	Deuteronomy 28:12	*Obey God and lend*
	Psalm 37:26	*Godly man lends*
	Psalm 112:5	*God blesses lender*
	Isaiah 24:2	*Buyer like seller*
	Jeremiah 15:10	*I have not lent*
	Ezekiel 18:7	*Restore pledge to borrower*
	Ezekiel 18:8	*Does not lend at interest*

Ezekiel 18:12	*Evil retains pledge*
Ezekiel 18:13	*Lends at interest*
Ezekiel 18:16–17	*Does not keep pledge*
Habakkuk 2:6–7	*Woe to those who lend at interest*
Luke 6:34–35	*Lend, expecting nothing*

INTEREST

Deuteronomy 23:19	*Do not charge interest to a brother*
Deuteronomy 23:20	*May charge foreigner interest*
Psalm 15:5	*Do not charge interest*
Proverbs 22:26–27	*Do not sign pledges*
Proverbs 28:8	*Wrong to lend at interest*
Ezekiel 18:7	*Godly returns pledge*
Ezekiel 18:8	*Godly does not charge interest*
Ezekiel 18:12	*Wicked keeps pledge*
Ezekiel 18:13	*Wicked charges interest*
Ezekiel 18:16–17	*Godly does not charge interest*
Ezekiel 18:18	*Ungodly extort from poor*

USURY

Leviticus 25:35–37	*Do not charge a brother usury*
Nehemiah 5:7–10	*Charging a brother usury*

Proverbs 28:8	*Usury will revert to God*
SURETY Genesis 43:9	*Surety for Benjamin*
Genesis 44:32	*Surety for Benjamin*
Exodus 22:26	*Return a pledge*
Deuteronomy 24:10–13	*Do not keep poor man's pledge*
Job 22:6	*Has taken a pledge from brothers*
Psalm 109:11	*Seize all a debtor has*
Proverbs 6:1–3	*Beg to be released from surety*
Proverbs 11:15	*Surety for a stranger*
Proverbs 17:18	*Ignorant becomes surety*
Proverbs 20:16	*Ignorant pledges cloak as surety*
Proverbs 21:27	*Sacrifice of wicked*
Proverbs 22:26–27	*Do not become surety*
Proverbs 27:13	*Take his garment*
PAYING DEBTS Genesis 38:20	*Judah paid harlot*
Deuteronomy 15:1–5	*Seven-year remission of debts*
Deuteronomy 31:10	*Year of remission of debts*
2 Kings 4:1	*Widow's children for debts*
2 Kings 4:7	*Elisha pays widow's debt*

Proverbs 3:27–28	*Pay when debt is due*
Matthew 5:25–26	*Make friends of lenders*
Luke 12:58–59	*Make friends of lenders*
Romans 13:8	*Do not be left owing*
Colossians 2:14	*Cancel debts*
Philemon 18–19	*Paul offers to pay debts*

RESOURCES

Books

Ron Blue with Jeremy White, *The New Master Your Money* and *The New Master Your Money Workbook*, Moody, 2004.

Howard Dayton, *Free and Clear: God's Roadmap to Debt-Free Living*, Moody, 2007.

Howard Dayton, *Money and Marriage God's Way*, Moody, 2009.

Howard Dayton, *Your Money Map*, Moody, 2006.

Ellie Kay, *Half-Price Living: Secrets to Living Well on One Income*, Moody, 2007.

Ellie Kay, *A Tip a Day from Ellie Kay: 12 Months' Worth of Money-Saving Ideas*, Moody, 2008.

James Meeks, *How to Get Out of Debt and Into Praise*, Moody 2001.

Dale Vermillion, *Navigating the Mortgage Maze*, Northfield, 2009.

Websites

Church Stewardship Resources — Brian Kluth: www.kluth.org

Crown.org — this site contains an abundance of helpful information and resources.

College Funding — Gordon Wadsworth: www.thecollegetrap.com

Credit Information: www.annualcreditreport.com

Debt Counseling and Assistance: www.financialhope.org

Investing Advisors: www.kingdomadvisors.org

Investing Funds and Resources: www.soundmindinvesting.com

Teaching Children: www.crown.org/children

More Helpful Information

For helpful articles on any of the following topics, visit Crown.org/Articles:

"Credit repair schemes"

"CCCS Offers Tips for Improving Credit Score"

Consumer Protection Act

"Dealing with creditors"

Fair Debt Collection Act

Fair Debt Collection Act: "The Fair Debt Collection Practices Act Part 2"

"Take Advantage of Free Credit Reports"

Taxpayers' Bill of Rights

"Your Access to Free Credit Reports"

NOTES

CHAPTER 7: BUD AND SANDI

1. http://www.stock-market-investors.com/stock-investment-risk/the-subprime-mortgage-crisis-explained.html

INTERLUDE: A QUICK HISTORY LESSON

1. http://www.getrichslowly.org/blog/2006/06/12/the-secret-history-of-the-credit-card/

2. http://articles.moneycentral.msn.com/CollegeAndFamily/CutCollegeCosts/How MuchCollegeDebtIsTooMuch.aspx

3. http://www.collegescholarships.org/loans/average-debt.htm

4. Ernest Istook, "The CRA Coverup," Oct. 15, 2008, The Heritage Foundation, http://www.heritage.org/Press/Commentary/ed101508b.cfm.

5. Press Release, Federal Housing Finance Agency, Sept. 7, 2008, http://www.treas.gov/press/releases/reports/fhfa_statement_090708hp1128.pdf

6. McKinsey Global Institute, "Will U.S. Consumer Debt Reduction Cripple the Recovery?, March 2009, http://www.mckinsey.com/mgi/publications/us_consumers/

7. News Release, Bureau of Economic Analysis, Personal Income and Outlays, August, 28, 2009, http://www.bea.gov/newsreleases/national/pi/pinewsrelease.htm (The personal saving rate dipped from 4.5% to 4.2 in July of 2009, but that figure still represented a significant increase in the saving rate over recent years.)

8. MarketWatch, "U.S. Consumer Credit Down Record Amount in July," Sept. 8, 2009, http://www.marketwatch.com/story/us-consumer-credit-down-record-amount-in-july-2009-09-08

INTERLUDE: THE BIBLE SPEAKS ON DEBT AND BORROWING

1. http://funny-about-money.com/2009/03/29/mortgages-is-a-30-year-mortgage-better-than-a-15-year-loan/

2. American Heritage College Dictionary, Fourth Edition (Boston: Houghton Mifflin, 2004), s.v. "surety."

3. Ibid.

CHAPTER 11: MORE ABOUT CREDIT

1. The three national consumer credit reporting agencies are:

Equifax: 800-685-1111; http://www.equifax.com

Experian: 888-EXPERIAN (888-397-3742); http://www.experian.com

Trans Union: 800-916-8800; http://www.transunion.com

2. Credit scores are available online at www.myfico.com for $12.95 or from Equifax (www.equifax.com).

3. See "Clean Up Your Credit Report Yourself," http://www.crown.org/LIBRARY/ViewArticle.aspx?ArticleId=351

4. "CCCS Offers Tips for Improving Credit Score," http://www.crown.org/LIBRARY/ViewArticle.aspx?ArticleId=209

5. http://www.crown.org

6. "Beware of bank overdraft-protection fees," http://blogs.moneycentral.msn.com/smartspending/archive/2009/04/22/beware-of-bank-overdraft-protection-fees.aspx

7. Ibid.

8. "The Fair Debt Collection Practices Part 2," http://www.crown.org/LIBRARY/ViewArticle.aspx?ArticleId=536

9. http://articles.moneycentral.msn.com/SavingandDebt/ManageDebt/Borrow$325PayBack$793.aspx?page=all

10. "Improving Your FICO Credit Score," http://www.myfico.com/CreditEducation/ImproveYourScore.aspx

11. "Seven Fast Fixes for Your Credit Scores" http://articles.moneycentral.msn.com/Banking/YourCreditRating/7FastFixesForYourCreditScore.aspx?page=2

CHAPTER 12: BILL CONSOLIDATION

1. Though there have been numerous changes to the tax laws since this act was passed, it still represents one of the most major revisions to tax laws in the history of the United States. You can easily find information about this law at http://www.taxfoundation.org/blog/show/1951.html as well as from other sources on the Internet.

CHAPTER 13: DEALING WITH CREDITORS

1. A form for listing debts can be found at http://www.crown.org/pamphlets/pdfs/DebtList.pdf as well as in *Family Financial Workbook* by Larry Burkett, Moody, 2000.

CHAPTER 14: LIVING WITH BANKRUPTCY

1. http://www.crown.org/LIBRARY/ViewArticle.aspx?ArticleId=577

PUBLISHER'S ACKNOWLEDGMENTS

Thanks to the team at Crown Financial Ministries for providing updates in keeping with Larry Burkett's original work, and for their continued commitment to helping Christians be reliable stewards of the Lord's material provision. Thanks to Tim Dekker and Ed Santiago for reviewing portions of the manuscript, and thanks to Joseph Slife of Sound Mind Investing for invaluable input on Bud and Sandi's story.

MONEY AND MARRIAGE GOD'S WAY

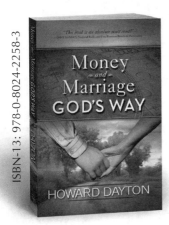

ISBN-13: 978-0-8024-2258-3

Money and Marriage God's Way will help you discover God's approach to growing your finances and strengthening your relationship with your mate. It highlights key issues such as debt, conflict, spending, investing, saving, and budgeting. Regardless of the books, magazines, or television programs you've seen, nothing compares with money and marriage *God's way.*

MONEY IN MARRIAGE WORKBOOK AND CD

ISBN-13: 978-0-8024-4230-7

Blending and sharing money with one's spouse is probably the most challenging aspect of marriage. It can be so destructive to a relationship or it can be a source of closeness. It's your choice. Recognizing that couples often bring into the marriage attitudes and habits about money, Larry Burkett uses this valuable workbook to identify each partner's tendencies.

MOODY
PUBLISHERS

MOODYPUBLISHERS.COM

HOW TO MANAGE YOUR MONEY

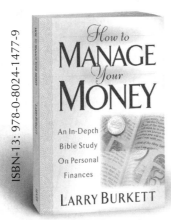

ISBN-13: 978-0-8024-1477-9

People often try managing their money apart from God's plan. Bad plan. Until people have an attitude change about money, it will continue to control and confuse them. *How to Manage Your Money* is an excellent tool to get readers on track toward a liberated financial life. This bestseller contains updated material, plus a step-by-step, in-depth study of God's principles for money management.

FAMILY FINANCIAL WORKBOOK

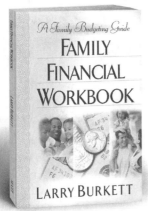

ISBN-13: 978-0-8024-1478-6

Finances are a significant cause of marital strife. Countless families give the false impression of being wealthy while drowning in a sea of debt. *Family Financial Workbook* is the best tool a family can have to manage their finances with God's direction. With a comprehensive collection of easy-to-follow worksheets, practicality is a key feature of this great resource.

MOODY
PUBLISHERS
MOODYPUBLISHERS.COM

MONEY BEFORE MARRIAGE

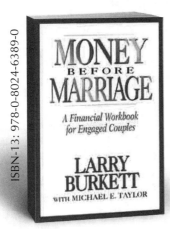

ISBN-13: 978-0-8024-6389-0

She's a shopaholic and he's a tightwad. Is their marriage doomed to fail? Should they even marry at all? It's been said that the two most destructive problems in a marriage are mismanagement of money and poor communication. Larry Burkett disarms these powerful threats by summarizing the key insights of wise money management. Learn how to avoid the most common financial and communication pitfalls experienced by thousands of newlyweds.

THE WORLD'S EASIEST GUIDE TO FINANCES

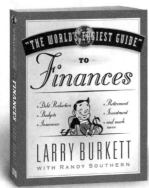

ISBN-13: 978-1-881273-38-7

Larry Burkett answers the call for a simplified, yet comprehensive guide to financial management. This book is a reference work that makes complicated terms and concepts easy to grasp with a touch of humor, and builds the confidence of a person of any experience level to understand and implement the information.

MOODY
PUBLISHERS
MOODYPUBLISHERS.COM

YOUR MONEY MAP

ISBN-13: 978-0-8024-6869-7

By revealing key biblical principles of finance, *Your Money Map* steers readers toward the clear biblical basics of money management through seven financial destinations that anyone can reach. No matter how distant the end goals may seem, *Your Money Map* provides realistic steps and all the necessary tools to achieve them. The end result? True freedom to invest your time and resources in furthering The Great Commission.

FREE AND CLEAR

ISBN-13: 978-0-8024-2257-6

Becoming debt-free may seem an impossible dream for many, but it is actually an attainable goal according to Howard Dayton, president of Crown Financial Ministries. He overcame his own struggle with debt by applying God's principles to managing his finances, principles he lays out in this practical, encouraging, never-give-up book.

MOODY
PUBLISHERS
MOODYPUBLISHERS.COM